Moby Dick

or

THE WHITE WHALE

Herman Melville

Adapted by Geraldine McCaughrean

Illustrated by Victor G Ambrus

Oxford University Press

Oxford   New York   Toronto

The Tattooed Harpooner

THERE is a whale in the sea, as white as a ghost, and it haunts me. It haunts me on winter nights, when the sky tumbles like a grey sea, and drifts of snow hump their backs at me. It haunts me in summer, when the sun overhead turns the grass sea-green, and the almond blossom rears up white over my head.

Sometimes, when I'm afloat in sleep, like a drowned sailor, he swims towards me — a nightmare all in white, jaws gaping, and I wake up screaming and salt-water wet with sweat. Somewhere out there in the bottomless oceans lives Moby Dick, a great white winter of a whale, and I shiver still at the thought of him. Even in summer.

Call me Ishmael. It might be my name. There again it might not. In my devout, church-going part of the world, it is usual for parents to name their children after characters in the Bible. Maybe mine did. There again, a man can always choose a new name, later in life, to suit his nature and experience. I call myself Ishmael, like that despised son of Abraham cast out into the wilderness places of the world. He may have lived apart from other men, but God was with him in the wilderness, even so, and heard him when he cried. *God hears.* That's the meaning of Ishmael. A man could be called worse. 'Ahab', for instance.

7

THE
SPOUTER

LANDLORD PETER COFFIN

That Ishmael in the Bible, he galloped about the wide world and never cared to settle down. I'm like that. I suppose that's why, finally, I took it into my head to go whaling. Five times I went to sea with the merchant navy, and then, for a change, I decided to go whaling. So I stuffed two shirts into a carpet-bag and went to Nantucket, because that's where you go to find a whaling ship.

9

It was late and bitter cold when I arrived, and the dark so dense that I could barely see where I was going. The creaking of an inn-sign led me to the door of a delapidated inn — The Spouter. Scribbled across the lintel in black letters were the words, *Landlord: Peter Coffin.* (A superstitious man might have taken that for a bad omen, but a man can't help his surname, can he?) In I went. 'Do you have a bed for the night?'

'If you don't mind sharing it with a harpooner,' said Peter Coffin, with a grin, and others nearby spluttered in their beer or looked me over and sniggered.

For all I had not been whaling before, I knew well enough about harpooners. They are generally very *big* men, not given to frill-fronted shirts or frock coats or taking tea with the ladies. I was nervous, no denying it. 'Which one is he?' I asked, peering round the bar. 'Maybe I'll look him over before I get under a blanket with him.'

'Not back yet. He's out trying to sell his head,' said the landlord, polishing a tankard.

I thought it must be the start of a joke. 'Oh yes?'

'Yes. He's sold the other four already, but he's out trying to get rid of the fifth . . . He may be a cannibal, but he pays regular. I don't judge a man beyond that.'

It was too late at night and I was too tired for such nonsense. So I took myself off to bed. But as I shed my top clothes and scrambled under the warm covers, I was feeling more and more nervous of who would come through the door and get into bed beside me. A madman, by the sound of it. Selling his head, indeed!

Beside the bed leaned the man's harpoon — a hollow metal spear with several ferocious barbs at the tip. I'm no weakling, but I would have been hard put even to lift it, let alone heave it at a passing whale. Just as I was dozing off, I heard footsteps on the stair. Best pretend to be asleep, I thought, so it was through my lashes that I first glimpsed Queequeg.

In one hand he held an Indian tomahawk — a lethal-looking axe — and in the other a shrunken human head.

His own face was hardly less ugly than the one in his fist, for it was tattooed with purple scrolls and black squares, and a single lock of hair swirled like a whirlpool in the centre of his forehead. When he took off his clothes, his body, too, was chequered purple-and-black, while columns of green frog tattoos trooped up and down his legs.

Out of a leather bag, he pulled a small brown object — I thought it was a human baby, at first, but it was a woodcarving of a crouching, hunched little man. Setting it down, he began to pray to it, his lips moving in a silent chant, his breath vaporous in the cold air.

'What a heathen! To pray to a carved idol!' I thought, as prim and supercilious as a Sunday-school spinster.

Then suddenly, Queequeg blew out the lamp, so that the room was plunged into darkness, and jumped into bed right on top of me.

'Whaahh!' I shrieked, rolling hard over against the wall.

'Who there?' His huge hands began to feel me like a blind pianist exploring a piano keyboard. 'Who you? What you do in my bed?'

'Coffin! *Coffin!*' I yelled.

'You speak or I finish you!'

'*PETER COFFIN!*'

The landlord burst into the room, thinking to find a fire or a ghost. His

11

lamp splashed us with yellow light. But when he saw me curled up like a hedgehog, and Queequeg trying to prise me open, he stood in the doorway and laughed out loud.

'Save me! Don't let him take my head!' I heard myself squealing.

'Bless me! What a row! Sorry, Queequeg: this fellow was in need of a bed, so I said he could share yours. Hcy! You! Queequeg won't do you no harm, sailor! Gentle as a moose, our Queequeg. Stop your racket and let the man get some sleep.'

An embarrassed silence filled the darkness after Peter Coffin had gone. 'I'm sorry,' I said. 'A misunderstanding.'

'No matter,' came his voice out of the darkness. 'You Christians give me plenty big frights some times.'

It turned out that he had not hunted the shrunken heads himself. He had bought them in New Zealand, to resell as curiosities to ghoulish Americans. He himself was a South Sea islander — a nobleman at that! His father was High Chief of the Kokovoko islanders. And shall I tell you something? That Queequeg proved a deal more civilized than many a man I've met before or since. By the time we had told each other our life histories and talked about the joys and terrors of the sea, I had made a friend I thought would last me a lifetime.

'Yojo says, you find us a whale ship,' said Queequeg next morning, pointing at the little carved idol. 'We two sail round the world.'

'I hope we can sign up together,' I agreed.

But Queequeg, as I found out, did not simply *hope* for the future to bring him things. 'We *will*,' he said, as if nothing else was possible, come good or ill.

12

I searched Nantucket harbour for a ship which took my fancy, and settled on the *Pequod* the moment I saw her. Besides being a rugged, sound, weathered little vessel, her entire ship's rail was studded with the teeth of whale she had taken, and in place of the bowsprit, the lower jaw of a sperm whale projected five metres. The tiller, too, for steering the ship, was the jawbone of a whale. It was as if the ship were kin to the beasts it hunted, or was gradually changing from wood into whalebone, from ship into whale.

Eager for my great adventure to begin, I leapt up the gangplank and generously offered my services to the man in Quaker-black sitting at a table on deck. 'Where do I sign, captain?'

'I'm not the captain. He's belowdecks, sick,' snapped the man in black. When he looked up at me, he had the face of a hell-fire preacher, sizing me up, saint or sinner. 'Starbuck's my name. First mate. Why dost thou want to sign?'

I was taken aback. 'I'd like to see the seven seas,' I said.

'Well, take a look yonder.' He pointed at the sloppy grey wash of the fog-bound sea. 'It all looks like that. Why put thyself to the pain of three years at sea and risk thy life whaling, to see more?'

'I've been on five voyages with the merchant navy — ' I began.

'Call that going to sea? Merchant navy indeed!'

'And I've heard so much about the whaling, that I've decided to try my hand at it.'

He gave me a look which seemed to write me off as a sinner determined to damn myself, then said, 'One three-thousandth share of the takings. That's all you get,' and turned the ship's register around, for me to sign.

'I have a friend,' I said, my pen hovering over the paper.

'What manner of friend? A three-year-three-times-round-the-world kind of friend?' blared Starbuck the mate.

'A harpooner, name of Queequeg. From Kokovoko Island.' I thought he might refuse to have a heathen aboard his ship, but as I looked at the names signed above mine, hardly a one looked American: Tahiti, Manx, Tashtego, Daggoo . . .

'Islanders make the best whalers,' said Starbuck. 'Maybe because the whale's a kind of island himself . . . Let him show his worth. this friend of thine, and he shalt sling his hammock alongside thee,' said Starbuck. 'We sail on Christmas Day.'

So, next day, I was back on the *Pequod*'s quarterdeck carrying my carpet-bag, and with my three-year-three-times-round-the-world kind of friend, Queequeg. The captain was still nowhere to be seen, but a lot more of the crew were in evidence. When they saw Queequeg's black-and-purple peculiarity, they were all set to jeer and scoff. But after Queequeg had thrown one man into the water and dived in to rescue him from drowning, he got more respect.

'You see streak of paint on bollard? That is eye of whale,' he said, weighing his harpoon in hand. (It was all we could do to see through the fog as far as the bollard on the dockside.) In a single, sudden, lithe movement, Queequeg raised and threw his harpoon. It hit the bollard with a thud, and vibrated with a single, hollow, eery note. When I ran ashore to fetch it back, I found the harpoon's barb had gouged away the fleck of paint altogether. 'That whale pretty much dead now,' boasted Queequeg from the bow.

I whistled with admiration. And it was as if my whistle woke the local ghosts, for a pale figure lurched out from between some stacked crates and bales, and came towards me cloaked in fog.

'I am Elijah!' he said, in a wavering howl.

16

'Good name for a prophet,' I said, feeling my face adopt that polite smile people reserve for idiots and madmen. 'Are you going to prophesy?'

'Have you seen him yet? Old Thunder?'

'Who?'

'Ahab, of course! The fiend Ahab!'

'Well, no, not yet. The captain's stayed belowdecks, so far. He's not been well, but we hear he'll be better before long.'

'The day Ahab gets better from what ails him, so shall this arm of mine!' Elijah shook the empty right sleeve of his coat. 'Sail not on the devil's business! For verily I say unto you, Ahab is a devil. I sailed with him once, and I know what I know! Is he not named with the name of wickedness? Was King Ahab not the wickedest man in all the Bible, who slew the Lord's prophets and worshipped heathen idols?'

'He can't help what his mother called—'

'Have you not seen the demons he keeps in his ship's hold? His work is Satan's work, and his brain is Satan's brain, and he goeth nowhere but unto Hell! Sail not with Ahab! I sailed with him once, and I know what I know!'

For a moment, my hair stood on end. Then a horse-drawn cart rattling along the wharf drew between us, and when it had passed, Elijah was nowhere to be seen. I hurried back aboard, in time to see Queequeg's name wrongly written into the ship's register: 'Quohog' it read. Against it was written 'one-seventeenth'—his share of the profits.

On a whaling ship, a good harpooner is more valuable by far than the likes of me.

2

The Gold Dubloon

SHIPS like the *Pequod* are not owned by one fat tycoon rubbing his soft hands in some New York counting house. Nor are they owned by their captains. Whole towns own them—a plank here, a nail there. Widows and retired sailors, clergymen and chandlers, thrifty shopkeepers and destitute orphanages may all own tiny shares in a single Nantucket whaler. So when it puts out to sea, a whole community of souls watches it go. They watch their investment sail over the horizon, and watch from the hilltops to see it sail home again: their means of survival. A lot was resting on the success of our voyage.

We sailed on Christmas morning, the sun still resting on the morning clouds like Jesus on his manger of straw. And still I had not set eyes on the mysterious Captain Ahab. He kept belowdecks, and the longer he remained invisible, the greater our awe of him grew. His cabin was like some holy shrine where no man entered—nor would have dared to enter, for fear of meeting God.

We heard him, though. At night, swinging in our hammocks, we could hear Ahab walking the deck overhead, up and down, up and down. A soft thud was followed by a sharp crack: a man's foot and then the sharp tap of a peg. For Captain Ahab had only one leg.

I heard Starbuck say to him once, 'Wilt thou not rest, captain? Thou wakest the men from sleep with the clatter of thy leg.'

The answer came back no louder than the growl of a sleeping bear: 'Why should they sleep? Do I sleep? Besides . . . the sound of my whalebone leg will trample dreams of whales into their sleeping brains, and what business have they to sleep unless it's to dream of whales?'

I looked around me, in the creaking, tarry dark. The words of the madman, Elijah, kept coming back to me. Who were the 'demons' Elijah had said were Ahab's travelling companions? These men snoring in their hammocks? Surely not. Exotic, yes, but demons? The meanest of the lot was the God-fearing Bildad, who knew every verse of the Bible, which gave him the excuse to be a skinflint. He gripped his moneybags tight to his chest and never spent a red cent if he could help it. Even now his head was resting on a pillow full of pennies. He deserved a stiff neck, but not to be called a demon.

Then there was Tashtego, whose glossy, purple-black hair was as long as a woman's: a pure-breed American Indian whose forefathers had hunted moose with bow-and-arrow.

Daggoo was a coal-black African, whose only wealth was the gold in his two huge ear-rings. Nobody in their right mind would have tried to steal them: Daggoo was as big as a bull and tall as a giraffe. But he was no demon.

There were men from the Azores, from Greenland, Shetland, and Wales, but though they were colourful barbarians, no one with an ounce of charity could have called them demons. I concluded that Mister Elijah was a half-wit and his talk of demons nothing but gibberish.

For three weeks, Ahab kept to his cabin. Then suddenly one day we looked up and he was there—above us on the quarterdeck—a long, lean man all in black but for the white of his whalebone peg-leg. His eyes barely showed, for the sockets had faced for so many years into sun and wind that they were screwed into a tangle of creases. The face was long and expressionless, like those monumental faces carved into the hillsides of Easter Island. Weathered into premature old age, Ahab's face was marred, too, by a scar which ran from the hairline down one cheek and in at the collar, as if it might run down as far as his feet. It looked as if our captain had been split in two and sewn carefully back together with needle and thread; or made, perhaps, from the halves of two different men. Inserting the tip of his whalebone leg into a hole in the deck, he perfected his balance, then leaned towards us over the quarterdeck-rail and bellowed, 'Tell me, men! What d'you do if you see a whale?'

'*Shout out, sir!*' we bellowed back at him.

'Then what?'

'*We lower the boats and go after him, sir!*'

Ahab looked ferociously gratified. He reached upwards, as if to snatch the trailing edge of a sail, but he had something in his hand. 'Here's an ounce of Spanish gold!' he declared. 'A sixteen-dollar piece! D'you see it? Mister Starbuck, pass me that mallet!' He placed the huge glittering coin against the main mast, as high as he could reach, and drove a nail through its soft, pure gold circle. 'This is for the man who wins me a certain white whale. You'll know it when you see it. It has a wrinkled forehead and a crooked jaw. There are three holes in its starboard fluke, and a twisted harpoon in its hump. That's mine, that harpoon.'

'I seen this white whale,' murmured Queequeg from close behind me. 'Last voyage. I put harpoon in, but he pulled loose.'

'I must have that whale, men! I will have him!'

'You mean Moby Dick, don't you, captain?' shouted Tashtego.

'Moby Dick, yes!'

'Wasn't it he that took thy leg, captain?' said Starbuck quietly from close by Ahab's shoulder, but Ahab answered as if we had all taunted him with the loss, and glared.

'Who told you that? Yes! He's the beast that took off my leg, and turned me into this stumbling cripple of a half-man . . . But now I'm part-whale, aren't I? Like him. Next time I'll make him pay. I'll chase him round the Cape of Good Hope and round Cape Horn, if I have to! We'll chase him from Norway to the Equator, and over all the sides of the Earth, till he spouts black blood. What d'you say, shipmates?'

It was thrilling talk. We were all on tiptoe, already looking out to sea, swearing death to the white whale as if it had eaten our own mothers. Sixteen dollars is a year's wage to most men, and each of us was inwardly spending that gold dubloon, cent by quarter. I know I was.

Only Starbuck, the first mate, had a look on his face like Low Sunday. Ahab saw it. 'What's your trouble, Quaker?' he growled, teetering slightly off balance. 'Too risky an enterprise for you?'

'Oh, I'll risk anything for enterprise,' said Starbuck. 'I'll follow the harpoon into the whale's mouth to be sure of getting its oil. That's my business. Oil. That's what we're here for. To turn a profit, taking oil. But revenge? Where's the profit in that? How many barrels of oil wilt revenge stow in the hold?'

Ahab rocked his big head from side to side and bared his teeth in a humourless grin. 'Oh, *money*! Is that what's worrying you, Mister Starbuck? Well, if money's the be-all and end-all, this planet of ours belongs to the book-keepers, and the stars are only hung up there to be counted and banked! But if it's any business of yours, Quaker, my revenge will make me richer *here*.' And he banged his chest.

Starbuck seemed more horrified than ever. 'Chase a dumb beast, to punish it for a crime it committed out of blind instinct? That's nigh blasphemous. It's mad, if thou ask me.'

Ahab swivelled round on his whalebone pivot, swelling with rage like a black sail full of wind. He jabbed at Starbuck with the fingers of both hands, his spittle flying in the man's face, his voice so loud that the mate winced and flinched away from it.

'Blasphemous? I'd pull the sun down out of the sky, if it insulted me!' roared Ahab. 'And that hulking fish insults me. Its very *existence* insults me. It's white, isn't it? Everything man fears is the colour of that whale. Ghosts, shrouds, masks; things invisible; blind things under the earth.

White's a zero. It's someone who ought to be there and isn't; a blind man's eye without a pupil in it; icebergs reaching under the water to claw the hull out of my ship. What is it out there, that lump of mystery? Do you know? Can you tell me? It's the *mystery* of him that screws me in knots. It torments me. He provokes me. I'm like a man in prison and he's the wall—the wall I have to smash down to get free! He's a white mask, and I don't know whose face is on the other side, laughing at me. Whose is it? Can you

23

tell me? Don't you understand anything? We have to smash away the mask. We have to *know*, d'you see? *All the answers.*'

The two men stood frozen, their faces so close they must have been breathing each other's breaths. Starbuck was pale—whale white with shock, bludgeoned half unconscious with words, like a man set upon by thugs. A wicked glint in Ahab's eye said that he knew he had Starbuck in his power, that they had locked horns and Starbuck had lost the trial of strength. The mate seemed to shrink, as if Ahab had shaken the very guts out of him.

Calling for grog, Captain Ahab summoned together the harpooners and filled the hollow shaft of each man's harpoon with neat liquor. He had them raise their harpoons, full of rum, in a toast. He had them raise the spears into a metal spire, with his own fist at the summit, joining them. His single, burning ambition conducted itself like lightning through those joined harpoons: '*Death to Moby Dick!*'

'Death to Moby Dick!' the harpooners chorused, round-eyed, like children dared into doing something huge and dangerous. 'And may God hunt us all to our deaths, if we don't hunt Moby Dick to his!'

I nearly shouted it myself, but the look on Starbuck's face made me think twice. Then someone thrust the grog bottle into my hand, and I drank off a swig. It hit my stomach like fire. It hit my brain like a fist. '*Death to Moby Dick!*' I crowed, and the little cook-boy Pip shook his tambourine in my ear and jangled away all my doubts. Here was a thing worth doing—to hunt a monster round the planet and rid the sea of it, like Theseus killing the Minotaur, like Perseus killing the Gorgon, like George killing the dragon. '*Death to Moby Dick!*'

The sun shone on the gold dubloon so brightly that I could hardly bear to look at it. Death to Moby Dick and sixteen dollars to me. No doubt about it.

Then someone started to dance, and soon we were all dancing, while Ahab, up on his quarterdeck, stretched out hands over us in a blessing. Or like the puppeteer pulling our strings.

The deck seemed a very different place a few hours later, when the crew lay sleeping in their hammocks and the sea shushed every other sound to a silence. Pip and I were on watch, down by the after-hatches, and had the job of hauling drinking water all the way from the central casks to the scuttle-butts on the captain's quarterdeck, ready for the coming day. There was nothing much left to talk about by then, and we came and went in silence, dropping the buckets down, hauling them back up.

'Listen!' said Pip all of a sudden. 'Hear that?'

'I didn't hear anything.'

'Someone breathing.'

'You're imagining things.' (We were at the opposite end of the ship from the fo'c'sle, where the crew lay sleeping.)

'Not me. I've got good ears, me! I can still hear it. Breathing. And a sort of chuntering, like a man talking in his sleep.'

The ship rolled on the swell. I steadied myself against the rail. Its whale-tooth studs dented my hand. I too thought I could hear it now: a snore — someone muttering in their sleep. Was the *Pequod* part-human now, as well as part-whale, that it breathed and snored and muttered in its sleep?

'It's that time of night. The sea plays tricks on you,' I told Pip.

'I've got good ears, me,' he said sullenly, and lugged his bucket away down the deck to the drinking barrel.

The moon, shining on the gold dubloon, was reflected in white lozenges all over the deck — as though the ship had leprosy and its hide was starting to turn a patchy white.

26

3

Ahab's Demons

I DON'T know what Ahab could have meant about the evil of whiteness. Say 'white' to me and I think of marble temples, apple blossom, knights on white chargers, weddings, lambs, and untrodden snow. Isn't it strange that one colour can mean such different things to two different people? Say 'white' to me, and I picture angels hovering in a Christmas sky, and stained-glass windows of Christ. The notion of a white whale spoke to me of one greater or better than the rest—the sacred white elephant among the common grey herd.

But then Moby Dick didn't bite off my leg. I can see that might change how a man feels about white.

There she blows!

A whale. Our first whale! My first whale! At the sound of the cry, Captain Ahab appeared on deck as if by magic. You would have thought we had sighted the lost city of Atlantis.

'Where?'

'Leeward! About two mile off, Cap'n! A whole school of 'em!' As Tashtego called down from the rigging, we saw for ourselves the next jet of water spurt, far off, like a leak in the seal between sky and sea.

Sperm whale blow as regularly as the striking of a clock. All we had to do was row towards the last spout and look out for the next. But as we struggled to lower the longboats into the water, our frenzied activity faltered to a halt. Out from under hatches at the stern of the ship leapt five figures we had never laid eyes on before. They came up like goblins from some underground den. Or pirates. We were panic-stricken.

But when they had leapt up the ladders to the quarterdeck, and mustered around Captain Ahab, we could see them for what they were. Extra whaling men. They had the sallow, yellowish skin of Filipino natives, which, even among the multi-coloured crews of Nantucket, made them a rarity. In my experience, Filipinos are only found aboard Christian ships working as spies.

One of them was older than the rest, with a single white tooth pushing out from behind his lips. His hair was hidden, or rather twisted into the coils of a white turban. White, yes. Now I think back to my first sight of Fedallah, I can see how white might become associated with evil after all.

Here were Ahab's demons, no doubt about it. Elijah on the dockside had not lied. And if he was right about the demons, what else had he told me that was true?

For a moment we stood staring at one another: the legitimate, hired crew and the secret, stowaway crew of which we had been told nothing. Then Ahab's impatient bellow set us a-flutter like pigeons.

'Lower the boats!'

Four harpoon boats instead of three hit the water. Four teams instead of three raised sail and leaned over their oars, in pursuit of the sperm whales. But Ahab's Filipinos—his hand-picked, crack crew of whale-killers—scudded ahead of the other boats. The rowers had such power in their arms that they could have outrowed a war canoe full of warriors. Watching them, a kind of jealous admiration stirred in us which did nothing to dispel our shock and suspicion.

'Those were the ones you heard breathing under the deck, Pip,' I said. 'Ahab's demons.'

'Demons? Pah! Just five more hands to help with the work, aren't they?' said Stubb, who was oars-master of my boat. 'What you griping about? Save your breath for rowing. Put your backs into it, men! Think we've got all day, or what? What you got in your bones for marrow? Weak tea? What you got under your sleeves for muscles, winkle shells? Sweat, can't you? Heave till your eyes stand on stalks. D'you think the whales are going to wait for you?' Stubb was a man who could pour out abuse and insults on his men all morning without ever repeating himself. He did it, mind, in such a tone of joking fun that no one ever took offence. We were already rowing fit to burst, as he well knew, closing fast on the pack of whale.

Ahab was leaning over the stern of the *Pequod*, directing the hunting boats like a general deploying his troops. But the Filipinos ignored his commands; they seemed to operate independently, on the orders of Fedallah alone.

Starbuck was master of my boat, standing in the stern, talking aloud to himself. 'The owners can't have known. The owners would never have given permission. He must be paying them out of his own gold. This is all down to the white whale.' But if it meant more whales would be killed, more whale oil stowed in the hold, more profits for the owners, who was Starbuck to complain? 'So long as he payeth for them, and not the owners,' Starbuck thought aloud, as we raced on through the wake of the Filipino craft.

The sky overhead was murky. There were snatches of mist and fog lying about on the sea like wool snagged from a flock of sheep. I scarcely noticed the weather. For I was about to encounter, for the first time in my life, the monstrous whale—a beast so huge that only the sea is large enough to house it. I was as thrilled as any cavalryman charging into battle for the first time.

And if the others saw the change in the sky, and felt misgivings, Starbuck silenced them saying, 'Plenty of time to kill a whale before the squall breaks.'

Queequeg stood in the bows with a harpoon on his shoulder, its rope coiling down into the bilges of the boat, at his feet. That rope would bind us to the whale if the harpoon found its mark. We were about to mine a mountain of meat, to plunder a mint of money, to strike oil in the middle of a million acres of water! What with Stubb driving us on, and the Filipinos taunting us with their speed, and Ahab's gold dubloon dangling in our brains, I think we all lost sight of the danger.

The school of whale disturbed the sea like a shoal of rocks just beneath the water. There was no white hump among them—nor was there any sight of the Filipinos, nor of Flask's boat, nor of Tashtego's. Believing we had outraced them and arrived first, we plunged proudly on towards that reef of whalemeat. Queequeg weighed the harpoon in his hand.

A sperm whale broke surface a stone's throw from the boat, and at the same instant we were smothered in spray. I naturally thought that the spouting whale, emptying the contents of its windpipe, had drenched us to the skin. But it was rain. At the very moment the whale breached, so did the clouds. Whale and squall and dense fog arrived at the selfsame moment. The heavens opened, and rain battered our eyelids shut. Queequeg threw his harpoon, the rope paid out, and the whale alongside us felt the sharp pang of a barb in its flesh. But Queequeg's hand was wet with rain and his grip had slipped. The harpoon only grazed the massive, shining flank.

Wind churned the sea into a confusion of sharp-topped waves. The whale we had tried to kill escaped back down into the weatherless dark of deep water . . . just as another rose directly beneath us.

The sail collapsed. Oars flew every which way. The air was filled with hot spray from the breaching whale, and we were lifted and flung into a creamy half-light of mist, spray, and breaking waves.

Miraculously, the keel did not snap. The planks did not crack. We did not even turn over! Though the boat was swamped full to the brim with water, it stayed afloat, submerged, and we sat on our benches watching

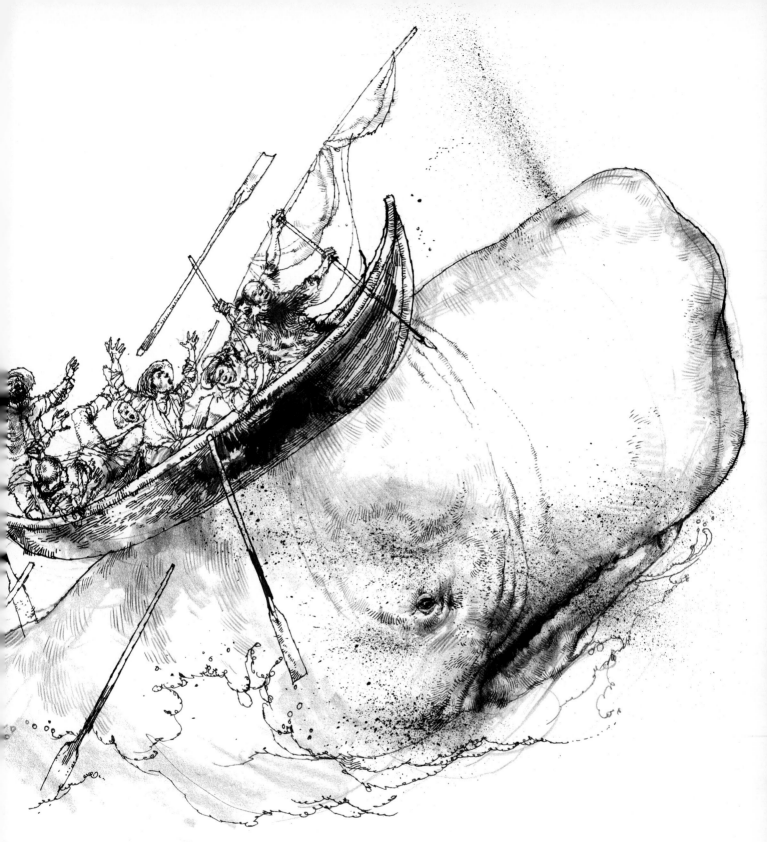

our trouser-legs wash about below the surface. The cold alone left us
speechless. Huge waterdrops hung in our lashes and rolled down our
cheeks, but no one was weeping: we were all too dazed to move a muscle.
The visible world round about us had melted into white fog. Even with

31

oars, we could not have rowed towards the *Pequod*, for we had not the least idea in which direction to row through the fog.

'My first whale, and it ends like this,' I said.

'First whale, fifty whale. Nothing special,' said Queequeg.

'You mean this often happens?' I meant to sound light-hearted, but it came out tin-hollow and a little hysterical.

'This ordinary,' replied Queequeg in his flat, unexcitable voice.

'This? This is nothing,' Stubb agreed. 'I've put out after whale, in a leaky boat, in the middle of a gale off Cape Horn,' said Stubb. 'This was nothing special.'

Where was everyone? We had no way of knowing. Were the three other longboats floating up-ended, just beyond the veil of fog? Were our shipmates floundering in the water nearby, or face-down, whale-watching? No sound reached us but the rain.

Night came down and held the fog to the sea. We were pinned beneath it, the freezing droplets clinging to our skin and hair, as disorientated as birds in a cloud. We could have been the last people on earth.

'If I had paper, I'd write my will,' I said.

'You got something worth leaving, then?' No one showed the least resentment that Starbuck had chased whale into the teeth of a squall. He was still held to be a prudent and cautious man, less likely than most to endanger his men.

'It's just the way things are,' said Stubbs to me. 'Sometimes we kill the whale. Sometimes the whaling kills us.'

'Only Ahab cannot accept and forgive,' said Starbuck from behind his praying hands.

It seemed impossible that the *Pequod* would find us in the fog. We could hear no flapping of sails, no voices hailing us, and though we shouted at first, our shouts were instantly trapped in the cobweb fog hanging round our ears. Soon we said nothing. The vastness of the ocean spread out all around, measurable only in days and weeks and points of latitude, not miles.

When dawn back-lit the mist, we were still sitting up to our waists in water. There was a strong temptation to lie down, pull the covers of water up over my head and to sleep. Not to be afraid any more.

Then I heard a loud hissing which I took to be the return of the whale, heaving itself out of the water to mow us down, force us under, finish us. A great dark shape loomed through the mist—it bore a sperm whale's jaw, too, studded with teeth.

'Jump, lads!' cried Stubb, and leapt over the side.

'We're under thy bow!' yelled Starbuck, rolling out of the boat with his hat clenched in his fist.

The *Pequod*, sailing out of the fog, accidentally ran down its own lost whale-boat. If it had passed to either side of us, by as much as a furlong, it would never have found us, and we would have stayed adrift on the sea everlastingly.

'God's hand hath saved us,' said Starbuck soberly, as we were helped aboard over the ship's rail. Myself, I was more inclined to throw my sodden boots in the air and dance about the deck to the music of Pip's tambourine. I was alive! Alive! Alive!

'What about the others? Was everyone rescued?' (I wouldn't have wished a night like that, even on Ahab's demons.)

But the other boats had wisely turned back sooner than us, and reached the *Pequod* before the storm broke.

The Filipinos had turned back the moment they saw no white hump among the grey. For Ahab's demons were employed to chase Moby Dick and nothing else.

4

The Kraken Rises

FEDALLAH was a holy man—but not of any religion God ever smiled upon. He told fortunes—looked into the future where no man ought to look, and saw there things which would turn a common man to stone. But Fedallah was no common man. He held himself above and apart from the likes of us—leastways that was how it seemed: always up above us, looking down. At night he climbed the rigging to the topmost stays, and gazed out at the sea, like an owl in the bellturret of a church.

'Who in his right mind keeps look-out at night?' we said to each other scornfully. 'No one but a fool keeps look-out at night!' But deep down, we were afraid, in case Fedallah could see things from his mast-top that were invisible to other eyes.

35

He was one of the few men admitted to Ahab's cabin. They would spend hours deep in discussion, Ahab's voice sometimes raised, but Fedallah's always the same low drone, as though he were chanting, or reciting, or conveying some memorized message carried in his labyrinthine brain. 'The cap'n's with his pet demon again tonight,' Starbuck would say, his face filled with revulsion. 'But which is the man possessed?' Fedallah had the power to spell-bind the captain in a way that running water can mesmerize a man and make him jump into it and drown himself. And however hard Ahab drove us, he let Fedallah do just as he pleased.

Sequestered in his cabin, Ahab pored over his charts, trying to divine the presence of Moby Dick in the featureless sea maps. Never far away from the door stood Starbuck, eaten up with anxiety for the welfare of ship and cargo. More at peace sitting in a boatful of icy water, lost in the middle of the ocean, when Starbuck was close to Ahab, his face was harrowed by worry, and he would mutter out loud. 'The man's obsessed. He's infected me with his obsession. Loathsome old man.' It was as though Starbuck were the harpooner and Ahab the stuck whale. Ahab's obsession was towing his first mate along in its wake, and Starbuck was powerless to break free.

Once, he found the captain asleep in his screw-base chair, a lamp clenched in one fist and a slide-rule in the other. A chart lay unrolled across his lap, and his face leaned into the lamplight, though the eyes were tight shut. 'Thou mad old man,' said Starbuck. 'Even asleep thou still searchest for it. Even thy dreams are full of white whale!'

We took other whales, of course: other spermaceti whales, Right whales, whales with humps purple like the Andes, brown as earthworks, and rock-grey monsters pocky with barnacles or whiskered with green sea grass. We killed them and winched them up alongside the ship, then harvested their blanket of blubber.

We boiled it down in great stinking witches' cauldrons on the deck, and poured off the oil into barrels—liquid wealth, liquid light. For the oil of whales lights a million lamps around the world. To us whalermen, those spouting islands of flesh are vessels carrying a cargo of light and warmth over the oceans, and we are the pirates trying to board, and seize the prize.

Not Ahab. No light or warmth lured him on along the sea-lanes. The whale he pursued was full of malevolence and wickedness—an iceberg so cold that, in touching it once, he had already burned the skin off his soul.

We sailed south, down the east coast length of South America,

towards the worst waves and biggest seas in the world. For hour after
hour, Ahab would stand on the quarterdeck, his ivory leg jammed into one
of the holes specially cut into the deck. Sometimes sleet or snow would
whiten his eye-sockets and seal up his very lashes, while overhead, we crew
hung from the mast in rope bowlines, watching for a sight of the whale.

South-east of the Cape, we sighted another whaler—the *Albatross*—
sailing homewards. Everything about her spoke of too many months at
sea, too many storms, too long bleaching in the sun and salt. Her sides
were white, ribbed with red rust, and all her sails ragged. She had been
whaling for four years.

The crew, too, were tattered and hollow-eyed—like skeletons
manning a ghost-ship. We passed close enough to see the skipper raising
his loud-hailer, just as Ahab was raising his.

'Ahoy there! Have you seen the White Whale?' was all Ahab had for
the *Albatross* by way of greeting.

The skipper leaned over the rail and was about to reply, when he
fumbled the loud-hailer and it slipped from his hand into the sea. He
shouted a reply, anyway, but without the hailer his words were snatched
away by the wind. He might as well have tried to toss breadcrumbs from
ship to ship. Ahab stood straining to hear, his hands cupped round his
ears, his face an agony of frustration. He would have lowered a boat, but
the wind was too strong, and carried the other ship past at full-tilt.

A shoal of little fish, which had been swimming in convoy with us,
chasing our keel, broke away from the *Pequod* and darted across to keep
the *Albatross* company on its homeward voyage. Ahab saw them go. You
would have thought they were mutineers jumping ship.

'Desert me, would you? You and everyone. Curse you, and good riddance!' Then he cupped his loud-hailer over his mouth and bellowed across at the *Albatross*, 'This is the *Pequod*, out of Nantucket, bound for round the world! If you reach home, tell 'em to address all our letters to the Pacific. And if we're not home in three years, address them to Hell!'

Round the world! I repeated it to myself. Round the world. What magic those words had to a young man thirsty for adventure.

'Thou'd not think he had a wife and little babe at home,' said Starbuck. 'Ahab? A child?'

'Yeah. A child of his old age. Apple of his eye. As mine is to me. Every day my dear wife carries my boy to the top of the hill behind our house. To look out to sea. Watching out for a sail. Watching out for me, see'st thou? There'll be a path worn to the top of that hill by the day I get back.'

I hung my chin in a loop of rigging and gazed out to sea. In the far distance, the Cape coast showed as a grey blur. It was a coastline strewn with the wreckages of ships—the carcasses of whales, too, cast up by storms. It occurred to me that some men give up more than others, to hunt the whale. Round the world for three years. How different that would sound, I thought, if I knew someone were climbing a hill every day to wave me home. Some men give up a lot for the sake of the owners.

'White whale!'

The cry went up as we ploughed north-east towards Java, through a bright yellow meadow of plankton. Ahab looked as if he would leap from the ship and run across the water on the dense, yellow carpet. When we

lowered a boat, he was the first into it, nimble despite his missing leg. We heaved the boat through the sea of plankton like beetles crawling through a field of wheat. The white hump in the sea neither spouted, nor rolled, nor changed position, but sank once and rose again in the same spot.

'Is it dead, d'you suppose?' I said to Queequeg.

'Not whale,' said Queequeg. 'Too big for whale.'

He was right. The longer we rowed, the larger the white hump grew. It was vast—larger by far than any monstrous whale.

The thing had no face, no mouth. Countless limp tentacles spread from its central core, coiling and twisting, floating and groping the water blindly: a Medusa of sea serpents, a miracle of vileness. If I live to be two hundred, I shall never see a sight so weirdly wonderful, so monumentally monstrous. It had no face, no eyes. It seemed to have no bone or rib or skull, but was one vast pulpy, undulating mass.

'What am I seeing?' I asked Queequeg, in a reverent whisper. But even he did not know, and the boats were full of men asking the same thing. 'What is it?'

With a soft, suck-chucking noise, the white thing sank from sight again, setting the surface of the sea quaking. It sank down and down until its whiteness disappeared in the depths.

'What was it?' said Flask to Starbuck.

The first mate was still staring at the empty expanse of water, his eyes wide with horror. 'I'd sooner have fought Moby Dick than seen thou, thou sea-ghost.' He met Flask's eye, and Flask flinched from the look in it. 'That, Flask, is what men call the Kraken. A legend. A thing I only half believed in before today. Biggest living thing in God's universe. They say it rises only to swallow ships or to die, and when it rises, it's a portent for the world of men. I found a single arm once, in the belly of the sperm whale, but I never saw the beast till now, nor I don't believe has any living man before us. Leastways not one who lived to reach port again and tell of it.'

We sat at our oars, overwhelmed by the strangeness of God's creation, overawed by the thought of that faceless, spongy monster below us.

'There's something for Ahab to tell his baby son,' I said nervously to Queequeg.

But Ahab was not even looking. He was already rowing back towards the *Pequod*. The whiteness in the ocean had not been Moby Dick and, in the instant he realized it, he had put about and lost all interest. The Kraken held no wonder for him. The ocean held no miracles. Nothing remained remarkable beneath the white moon but Moby Dick and Ahab's hatred. Alongside Ahab's hatred, the Kraken was a piece of cuttlefish hanging in a birdcage—a minor irrelevance, a digression from the *Pequod*'s true quest. An irritating delay. Nothing had the power to move him any longer, but the one obsession which had turned his soul, like his leg, to ivory.

'Have you seen the White Whale?'

Every ship we sighted, every crew we hailed, Ahab hailed with the same question. 'Have you seen the White Whale?'

Some had not. Some did not even believe in Moby Dick—a legend, they said, or a dozen different pale whales called by the same name. Some had seen him, but two years before, and on the other side of the world.

Captain Boomer, an Englishman, had seen him more recently. A year before, on the Equator, they had met, and Boomer was as well acquainted with the White Whale as Ahab himself, for just the same reason.

'You'll forgive me if I shake left-handed,' said the Englishman, when he came aboard at Ahab's eager invitation. Our two ships floated at anchor, a furlong apart, like dancers too shy to touch.

'Was it Moby Dick took off your right arm?' asked Ahab eagerly.

'It was.'

'Then let me shake that empty sleeve of yours! A one-legged man greets a man with one arm. Tell us how it was!'

So Captain Boomer, of the whaler *Samuel Enderby*, recounted his own lost battle with Moby Dick—how the harpoon had struck home in the whale's jaw but the whale had turned and spat it out, like a salmon despising the fisherman's hook.

'His fluke caught the boat. An old harpoon from some other whaler was still sticking out from the tail, rusted home solid. The iron snagged me in the arm, and I knew then and there I was a maimed man.'

'It was mine! That was my harpoon!' cried Ahab, proud rather than sorry. 'So now you're hunting it round the world, eh? Like me! To make it pay!'

Captain Boomer downed some rum and laughed as he shook his head. 'Not me! Isn't one arm enough? I can't spare any more. There'd be plenty of glory in spiking Moby Dick, I don't deny that. But you can't stir your tea with glory, can you, nor walk to church on it.' He smiled: a warm, agreeable smile born of a gentle nature. He was a man at peace with himself. 'No, he's best left alone, that White Whale, to die of old age.'

He might just as well have spat in Ahab's face.

The ivory leg squealed on the deck as Ahab turned his back on Boomer. It skidded, struck against a capstan, and jarred with such force that there was a loud cracking sound. 'Best left alone? Isn't everything worth having? Since Adam ate the apple in the Garden of Eden, hasn't that been the only thing worth chasing? The thing that ought to be left alone? Fool! Spineless coward! Well, I mean to fight Moby Dick or die in the attempt. I'm not afraid of looking him in the eye! Get off my ship, you! I've got no more time to waste on gutless cripples like you. I've business to attend to!'

Captain Boomer set down his glass, as though the rum in it had turned very sour. 'Then I hope, for your crew's sake, that you never find what you're looking for, Cap'n Ahab. Good-day to you.'

43

5

Pip Jumps

POOR creatures. I got used to the smell of their death, but I never quite accustomed myself to the pity of it.

There they are, roaming through the sea with all the majesty and might they had on the fifth day of the world, when God placed them in the brand new oceans. They spout hot spray at the sky, and feel it fall again on their mountainous backs, while little servile fishes preen their louvred gills, and barnacles cling grimly on, as we do to our moving planet.

Then all of a sudden, a strange wooden beast hoves into sight—round-bellied and about the size of another whale. As if it were giving birth to a pup, it looses a small version of itself, which hurries over the water, closer and closer, until it fills the sight of one eye. A puny, insignificant creature stands up into view and hurls a pin, a metal toothpick, attached to a length of thread. A blinding pain. A blindness. And the whale is dead, killed for its blubber.

What once moved as a beautiful, buoyant, island realm is winched up by its flukes—a dead weight so huge that the mother ship heels dangerously over. The head is sawn off—a third of the whale—and slung over the ship's other side, to counterbalance the great weight of the remaining carcass. Then fat and flesh are flayed from the stinking hulk with blubber hooks and whale spades.

Shark rush in from every horizon. Like jackals rejoicing in the death of a lion, they dart towards the smell of blood, and gorge themselves in a frenzy on whatever they can reach, leaping to snatch in vain at tastier parts beyond their reach.

Down in the fo'c'sle, we used to hear their flanks and tails bang against the ship's bottom as we and the sharks fed. What did we eat? Well, whale meat, of course, same as the sharks! Our cook-boy Pip fried it in a pan as black and round as his own face. And while the sharks outside rent to shreds whatever they could reach of the trailing carcass, we bent our heads and shovelled the same into our hungry mouths. At first, the stench put me off my food, but after a few weeks' whaling, I worked up as good an appetite as the next man. Smell a smell for long enough, and it stops troubling you.

Young Pip. It makes me smile, just calling him to mind. Do you know anyone like that? His mouth was always open in a wide, white grin, and he sang every moment he was not sleeping. We grumbled about the toughness of our whale-steaks, we talked of casting him adrift if he didn't learn to cook better; we mimicked his Alabama accent. But Pip just laughed, and skipped his bare feet over the splintery deck and sang songs as though he was too full of song to keep them all inside. Fourteen he was when we set sail from Nantucket, and somewhere along the way I expect he turned fifteen, though the plantations where he was born don't pass out birthdays to the likes of Pip: he was born a slave.

In fact, he was so happy to be a free boy, out on the great unshackled ocean, that he never objected to tossing our whale steaks or scraping the decks or scrubbing the cauldrons, or playing his tambourine. When captain or crew cried 'jump', Pip jumped, he was so eager to please. Poor creature.

Fedallah, on the other hand, strove to please no one. He did as he chose, keeping his midnight watch from the mast top, sleeping away the heat of the day. 'Who but a fool keeps a watch at night?' we said.

45

'There she blows! The White Whale!'

I thought at first, that I had dozed off to sleep and dreamed it. Then we heard Ahab's ivory leg clatter across the deck above, and he was bawling for us to turn to. I shook Queequeg's hammock to wake him—but it was empty. Sensing (as he always did) when something was about to happen, he was already on deck, while the rest of us collided on the ladder, and emerged on deck shivering in our shirts and bare legs.

'Guess he's seeing things now, the mad devil,' I said hopefully to Queequeg, but he shook his head.

Fedallah hung way out from the rigging, over the oil-black sea, his finger pointing. There, on the moonlit horizon, a geyser of silver spray rose, fanned out, and drifted in veiling spray. We scrambled into the rigging for a better look, and as we gained height, the palest of outlines became visible beneath the surface of the sea, where the plume had spouted. A reef? Or a reflection of the Milky Way? Then the spout came again and there was no doubting it—a white whale, and within half a mile.

Ahab was on his quarterdeck shouting commands, fully dressed, of course—I don't believe he any longer even went to bed, for all the sleep it brought him. There was a gleam in his face like new love.

'Raise the sails! Up! Up! Steer for the spout. Lay on more canvas, I said! Put your backs into it! *Put on more sail*, damn you!'

Again the whale spouted.

We heeled towards the fountain of glistening spray—a sight so beautiful that grown men gasped. Three times the whale showed us its white cockade of water, as white feathers waved at cowards to taunt them. The sight certainly taunted Ahab. 'Make after him, why don't you!' We bore down on the spot as fast as sail and wind would carry us.

Then it was gone. No repetition. Whichever whale we had seen, it had gone deep. By the time we crossed the spot where the white whale had spouted, the water was of no more remarkable a colour than any other furlong of night sea.

We wondered, then, why we had doubted Fedallah's sanity. He had not been simply looking out for whales: he had been looking out for Moby Dick. And, of course, that gleaming white bulk had shown through the black swell.

Fedallah spent all morning in Ahab's cabin, whispering behind locked doors, and I thought (like a good Christian), why does the captain persist in wanting to know more than God meant him to know? Why does he listen to that *fortune-teller*? Then I turned to Queequeg and said, 'Was it really Moby Dick? Will we see it again?' I simply had to know.

Looking back, I see now that I, too, was desperate to glimpse the future; that I, too, had my own personal prophet of sorts. Queequeg's uncanny ability to *know* things ahead of time made me feel less vulnerable to sudden, nasty shocks. Living from day to day, well, it's like feeling your way along a dark passage, trying to guess what lies round the next corner, hoping nothing too horrible will leap out of the shadows. Why does God keep men guessing like that?

Queequeg sat sharpening the barb of his harpoon, the tattoos on his face scribbling out all expression. 'Tonight,' he said. 'He will come tonight.'

So he did. And the night after, too.

At the selfsame hour on the second watch, Fedallah cried out from his mast-top perch, and again the snowy fountain of glistening spray blew in shreds across the moonlit sea.

'He beckons me onwards,' murmured Ahab on his quarterdeck, but we all heard him. 'Moby Dick beckons me onwards to the Last Battle. Well, lead on, brute! I'll grasp you yet.'

His hands reached out involuntarily in the direction of the whale-spout, and closed on the empty air. He thought, I'm sure of it, that he was King Arthur reaching for silver Excalibur. If he could once close his fist round that plume of spray, he would inherit such powers, such dominion . . . Suddenly, I noticed my stomach cramp, as though someone were holding me tight by the lights. And I realized that, like it or not, I was a part of Ahab's quest. So was every man aboard. We were his company of knights within the tiny kingdom of the *Pequod* and he could send us out to fight whatever dragons or monsters threatened his dominion.

One day, Stubb's after-oarsman sprained his hand and could not row. He was sinking a spade into a dead sperm whale when he struck bone—as a man digging a garden bed might strike a rock. It jarred his wrist and elbow so badly that he was no more use in the row-boats than Captain Bloomer would have been with his one hand.

'Pip shalt go in his place,' decreed God-fearing Bildad who, as a part-owner, did not want a penny profit lost because of a boat short-handed.

So Pip was put into the boats. Little Pip. He was small for his age, and as he was lowered down the ship's side, he looked no more than a little boy, rigid with fright. His lips were pursed over his big white teeth: no smile. But the rims of his eyes showed white instead, around the brown iris. He was born into slavery, and put up no kind of protest or plea for pity. But poor Pip. We could all see he was terrified. The knuckles of his black hands showed white as he gripped the oar.

The blade flailed. He missed the water and fell off his bench. He dug too deep and dropped his oar. But Stubbs, rather than heaping insults and abuse on him, in his usual way, only told him to be a 'good, brave boy,' and to do his best.

The first outing, Pip did nothing wrong, and the smile crept back to his lips. But the second time we gave chase to a whale, things did not go so smoothly. We were after a Right whale—so called because it swims slow and floats when it's dead, which makes it the 'right whale to hunt'. Tashtego threw his harpoon, and it struck, good and sound, behind the eye. The whale—as whales will—gave a twitch, and thrashed its tail against the bottom of the boat; it happened to hit the boards directly under Pip's seat. Thinking the boat would be smashed to pieces, he leapt up in terror— clean over the side, taking with him a length of the harpoon rope as it began to pay out. The whale bolted, the line went taut. It coiled tight round Pip's chest and neck, and his lips turned instantly blue as he was towed along, sometimes above water, sometimes below, caught in a knot somewhere between the running whale and the boat it was towing.

'Wretched boy!' yelled Tashtego, drawing his knife. He glanced at Stubb, who hesitated for a moment. He liked Pip. But there again, the whale was big. The profits from it would be good. Boys are two-a-penny.

'Cut!' ordered Starbuck, from the middle of the boat, and Tashtego cut through the harpoon rope. The whale escaped. Pip was saved. But by God! we cursed him for losing us the whale! Starbuck pulled the boy out of the water by his shirtfront and bellowed in his face. 'Doest that again, boy, and I shalt leave thee to drown, I promise thee! We've had precious few whales this voyage, without we have to give one up for the likes of thee! We'll cut no more ropes for thee, dost comprehend me?'

I liked Starbuck the better for giving the order to cut. Oh, we swore at Pip when he was safe and dry on board the *Pequod*, but we were all fond of him. Yes, I liked Starbuck the better for pitying Pip.

The next time it happened, Starbuck was not in the boat. A whale's tail slapped the bottom of the boat . . . and Pip jumped. This time, he did not foul the rope. But the whale bolted, the rope grew taut, and the whale-boat started its headlong ride in the wake of the running whale. Stubb had seen Pip jump. He remembered Starbuck's words. He saw Pip in the water, saw that he was not entangled in the rope, knew that there were other of our boats in the vicinity. And he gave no order to cut the rope. So the whale-boat sped away, leaving Pip in the sea, screaming after it, 'Don't leave me! Please don't leave me!'

It took three miles for the harpooned whale to tire. Meanwhile, Pip bobbed in the ocean, beneath a viciously hot sun, sobbing salt tears into the saltier sea. None of the other whale-boats did chance upon him. He was adrift and forgotten.

Now Pip was not a stupid boy. He had imagination in plenty. He had seen the Kraken, the devouring sharks, the myriad breeds of fish emptying

from the stomach of a dead whale. He had heard talk of Moby Dick. And all these creatures were living in the sea below him—millions of mouths, tendrils, tentacles, and teeth; drowned sailors, wrecked ships, the souls of little cook-boys and a million other undiscovered things, washing, washing, washing to and fro.

It so happened that, eventually, the *Pequod* herself spotted Pip. Ahab saw the small black head bobbing, and ordered ropes to be dropped down from the ship's rail, to haul him aboard. So Pip was saved from the ocean a second time.

But by then, his wits had all washed out of him, as salt washes out of soaked meat. His body was rescued, but a part of his spirits had sunk, down and down, into a depth of ocean from which no grapples or hooks could ever fetch it back. As he was pulled up, the captain bent and offered him a hand. Little Pip, imagining himself dead, and ecstatic at the touch of a human hand, the sight of a human face, believed he was meeting God in person.

He clung to Ahab's good leg, worshipped and adored him, stroked him, gazed at him with eyes full of rapture, sang snatches of hymns, and shuddered uncontrollably in the grip of shock. It was farcical, but nobody laughed. It was terrible, but no one led the child away to the peace and rest of his hammock.

From that day onwards, Pip trailed about the ship after Ahab—would not be parted from him—holding a corner of his jacket or even his hand. Ahab, far from kicking him away, showed him an utterly uncharacteristic gentleness. The whale has its cleaner-fish. The king has his jester. Lear had his fool. Now Ahab had Pip—'Wise master! Wonderful master!'—who glorified him with praise from morning till night. 'D'you know what I see'd, Lord, when I was in the sea, Lord?'

'What did you see, Pip?'

'I see'd your foot working the treadle of the world, Lord! Making the planets spin round and the stars to fly and the oceans to pull to and fro. Rockety-rock, rockety-rock. Your foot on the treadle in the bottom of the sea, Lord! Making the world roll on, Lord! What a wonder you are! Hallelujah!'

When Starbuck found Pip sleeping across the threshold of Ahab's cabin, like a dog, in his distress he struck out at Pip and jarred his head with a slap. At the top of his voice, he quoted the Bible at him: *'Thou shalt have no other god before me! Nor shalt thou set up any graven image or idol in place of the Lord thy God!'*

Pip stared at him, his eyes white-rimmed with fright. 'Won't, sir! Honest I won't! Only him. He my only wonderful god, sir, on land or sea. Only captain god, sir!'

'Poor child. I can't see what harm . . .' I started to say, in defence of Pip's poor head.

Starbuck raged back at me. ' 'Tis not Pip's blasphemy I'm afraid of, sailor! He's just a poor, damaged wretch! No, 'tis Ahab himself I fear for, cast in the role of God! I do believe he finds it suits him. The man thinks he is above the rule of Divine Law! The man thinks he *is* Divine Law! The man's—'

He stopped short of calling Ahab mad in front of me. He was first mate, after all. All the rules of the sea forbade him to criticize his captain in front of a common sailor. And Starbuck was a stickler for the rules. A first mate must obey his captain as a slave obeys his owner, as an archangel obeys the word of God.

Anything else is mutiny, isn't it?

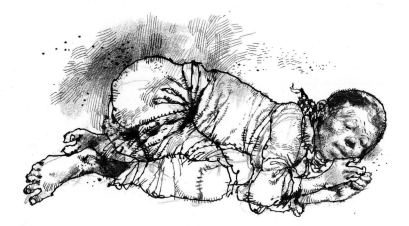

6

Ambergris

AFTER the boiling down, lumps of blubber still float about in the whale oil like dumplings in a stew. They have to be broken down by hand. It is delectable work. I loved it, squelching and squeezing the lardy in my fists, feeling it ooze out between fingers and thumb. I suppose you think a sailor's hands are always calloused and rough? Not ours. After that squeezing, we had hands like ladies, hands softer than any idle gentleman who never pulled on a rope in his life.

We had light, too. While most seamen blunder about below decks like blind moles—no expensive oil lavished on lighting lamps for the likes of them—we whalermen are a different breed. Our whole world ran with whale oil, so the *Pequod* blazed with lights from stem to stern after dark: a beacon on the night sea.

The darkness in Ahab, on the other hand, increased with every passing day.

The striking of his peg leg against the capstan had split the ivory, and gradually the splits began to open. In the end, he had to order the ship's carpenter to carve him a new leg. Chippy confided to us afterwards what Ahab had said—how he could still feel the lost limb, as though it had never been amputated, feel every toe, every muscle, every intricate joint, every hair in its follicle. The pain in that phantom leg kept him awake at night; the flatness of the bedclothes taunted him, for he could *feel* the leg and foot which ought to make a mound in the blanket.

It woke in me a pity for the old man, but chiefly it made me wonder what else Ahab could sense which was no longer really there. Moby Dick, for instance. Perhaps Moby Dick, like Ahab's leg, was also dead and gone, floating on its back somewhere, decomposing into food for the fishes, into pieces of floating white lard, its bones sinking down to the ocean bed. All things decay in the fullness of time . . . I could almost smell the stink of the old white monster breaking up.

Beside me, Queequeg gagged, and I realized that the smell was not in my imagination at all, but all about me. We had sailed into a cloud of unbearable stench.

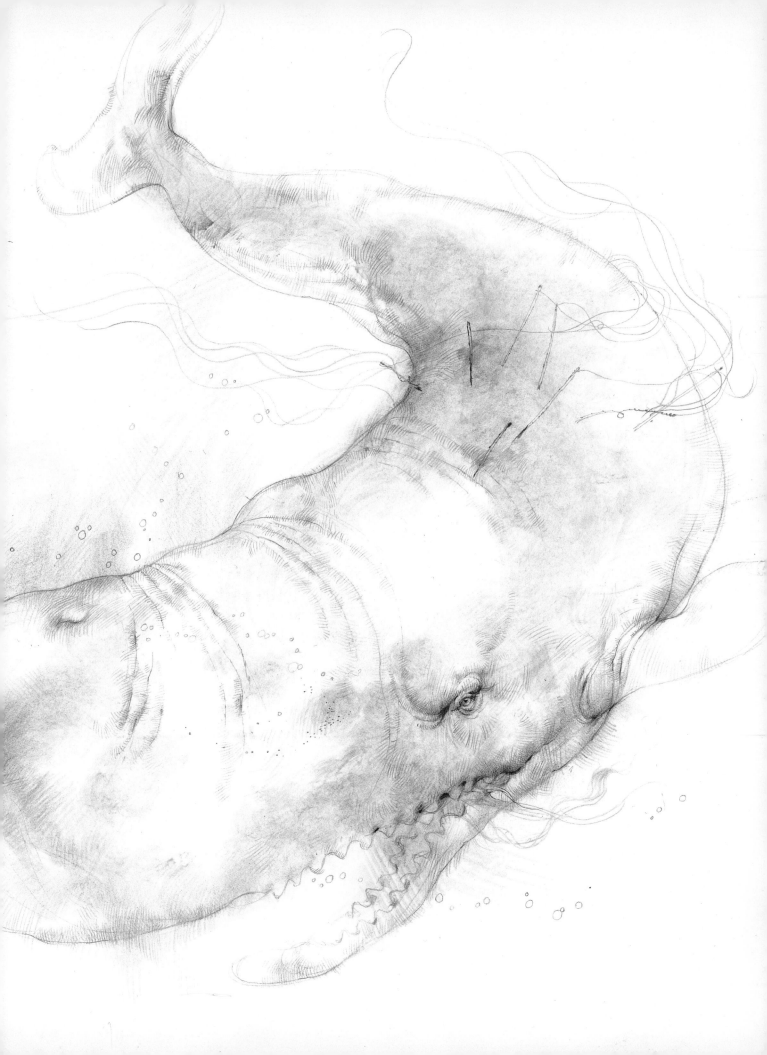

'Have you seen the White Whale?'

So eager was Ahab for news of Moby Dick that he was ready to draw alongside a French merchantship called *Le Bouton de Rose* even though she had two dead whales in tow behind her. One was the beast which had escaped after Pip jumped the first time. Maybe the wound our harpoon made had festered and killed the poor brute. In any case, Stubb believed the whale ours by right, and he took steps to get it back.

'Are you mad? Towing dead whales?' he shouted across the gulf between ships. 'Don't you know that's a sure way to catch whale fever?'

'"Whale fever?" We never before hear of this sickness!' called back the French mate.

'Truly? Well I never! Only last week we hailed a ship with nine crew dead from messing with dead whales!'

'What's he after?' I asked Queequeg. 'That whale's so shrivelled up, it'd give less oil than my Aunt Bessie.'

'Ah, not oil! Maybe something better,' said Queequeg. 'Treasure your Aunt Bessie kill for, maybe.' Taking me by the hand, he ran me down the length of the ship, like a child towards Christmas. He thrust a whale spade into my hands, and grabbed one himself.

Meanwhile, the French, with much spreading of hands, tearing of hair and whiteness of face, cut loose the dead whales and *Le Bouton de Rose* fled, like a convict loosed from his ball and chain. The French captain was in the middle of calling to Ahab what he knew of the White Whale—a sighting—a rumour of a sighting. Suddenly, the distance between them widened and the Frenchman's words fell short of the *Pequod*, along with his thanks for Stubb's kind and generous warning.

No sooner was *Le Bouton de Rose* over the horizon than we lowered the row-boat, climbed in, and crossed to the floating hulk of the dead whales. The smell was as thick as a swarm of flies. Every man on the *Pequod* with a pipe to his name had crammed it with tobacco and surrounded his head with clouds of sweet tobacco smoke, like a horse with its head deep in a nosebag. Anything, to keep off the stench.

We boarded a carcass that was floating on its back—like men claiming an uncharted island for king and country. The belly-skin underfoot was wrinkled and blackening. Where the broad belly began to narrow into the tail, Stubb sank in his spade—a pirate on a treasure island looking for the spot marked X.

'Leave that!' came Ahab's voice from the ship.

'A few minutes, Cap'n!' Stubb returned, heaving a spadeful of india-rubber blubber into the sea. He opened up a trench, a pit, a mine, digging his way into the creature's guts.

'Leave it, Stubb!'

'But the ambergris, sir! I think I can—'

Panting and grunting with exertion, Stubb went on digging. I too was fired with the desire to dig, though I had no idea what ambergris was or whether I wanted to find anything that hid itself in such an unwholesome place.

'I've no time for your treasure-hunting!' bellowed Ahab, and under his breath Stubb poured out the same stream of invective he generally reserved for his oarsmen. *What's his hurry? To be early for his funeral?*

Mad old villain. Crazy old man. What's he out here for, if it's not to get rich? What kind of a whalerman turns his back on a chance of ambergris? Does he think we won't share it with him? We'll share it out fair and even, Cap'n!' he shouted back across the water, baring his teeth in an ingratiating grin, then went back to muttering as he dug. '*Why don't he smoke on his pipe and stop up his mouth? What's his great hurry to stay poor?*'

'Stubb, I'm warning you!'

'We find ambergris, we all rich, sir!' cried Queequeg, while beside him Stubb nodded in exaggerated agreement and mimed triumph and great wealth in his attempt to make Ahab understand.

Queequeg went down on his knees so suddenly that I almost hit him with my spade by accident. He plunged a hand deep down the dug hole into the guts of the whale, and his fist closed round a silvery substance. Instantly, a perfume plumed from the stinking hulk so beautiful that it transformed our carcass island into Cleopatra's barge.

'Ambergris!' cried Queequeg, and rubbed it over his shaved head.

Stubb fell on his knees and scrabbled out two fistfuls of the treasure. 'Ambergris!' he gasped. 'Most precious stuff in all God's creation. Give me a pot—something to put it in!' Now Ahab would have to let him stay and finish the job.

Here were the makings of a thousand bottles of perfume, ten thousand fragrant lady's throats inviting men's kisses, dabbed with lard from the guts of a rotting whale. It was like some joke perpetuated by God during the days of Creation. I could almost hear him saying to his angels: 'Let us hide this where they will never think to look.' It made me laugh out loud. It made me laugh myself breathless. But laughing did not stop me

getting down on my knees and grubbing for my share of the silver ambergris, while Stubb, in his imagination, shared out the proceeds of our incredible windfall.

'We'll all be rich men! We can turn for home now! If there's enough here, we can sail straight for home!'

'Stubb, I won't tell you again!'

'But Cap'n! It's *here! There's ambergris here! Look!*' He held up fistfuls, like a miner who has struck gold.

'You've spilled enough of my time already! The day's wasting. Get you back aboard or I'll maroon you where you stand, you and your cannibal friend!'

He meant it. He was giving orders for the sails to be unfurled, for the sea anchor to be raised. Ahab really meant to leave us adrift on the rotting whale, in the middle of the sea, sooner than delay his whale hunt by so much as one hour. Bleak weeks and months he had waited, chasing a ghost from Atlantic to Pacific, and yet one morning was too much to spare for a harvest of precious ambergris.

We took such as we could carry in two hands, and stepped back into the row boat. To row, we had to lay it down in the bottom of the boat, and by the time we re-reached the *Pequod*—our brains reeling with the heady perfume—such ambergris as we had salvaged was washing around the wet bilges like so much frogspawn.

'The man wants us all to die poor,' said Stubb bitterly, and I thought I could hear tears in his throat—though it may just have been terror at the thought of being left behind.

The crew seethed at the loss of their share in the ambergris. They gathered at the taffrail and muttered as they watched the twin carcasses drop away to stern, their treasure lost to the pecking gulls and sipping fish.

Starbuck, the mate, took the loss better than most. Perhaps his Quaker soul shrank from sudden, easy, wonderful wealth, and he believed a man should only grow rich by good, honest, back-breaking toil. Even so, when next day the oil drums in the hold began to leak, he was the first to deem it a disaster.

'May it please thee, sir, give the order to heave-to!' he called, as he ran towards the quarterdeck and climbed the ladder to reach Captain Ahab. I never saw Starbuck shift so fast, and it made me realize that beneath the black garb of his religion, he was still a young man. 'Some of the barrels are leaking, sir! They must be brought up above decks and repairs made!'

'Make 'em as we go,' said Ahab, without so much as turning his eyes

from the sea. His weathered face was so hardened against the wind and spray that he seemed like a statue cast in brass.

'I cannot!' protested Starbuck. 'Every man must needs set to and empty the hold, and the barrels must be stacked on a steady deck or we shalt lose them over the side!'

'Then leave 'em where they are and to hell with the leaks,' snarled Ahab. 'I'll not lose a day tinkering with barrel hoops like some street-corner grocer!'

'Then thou shalt lose more oil in a day than was gained in a year!'

We crew broke off from what we were doing, our hearts in our mouths, at hearing Starbuck directly contradict the captain. 'We are come twenty thousand miles for this, sir! And must we lose it now?'

Ahab's eyes widened and his fist clenched. 'Indeed we have! Twenty thousand miles!' he sighed to himself. 'And we almost have it in our grasp!'

'I meant the *oil*, sir. The oil leaking in the hold.'

'Bah! Let it leak. The world's full of leaks. The days of my life are leaking away out of me. I don't see you stopping to plug up that leak. No, damn you! I'll not heave-to!'

'And what wilt the owners think to that?'

'Damn the owners!' blared Ahab. 'Owners of what? They don't own me and they don't own this ship—not while I'm captain of her! The only owner a ship knows when it's on the high seas is her captain, and while I'm in command, *I* own the *Pequod*, and the bodies and souls of every man aboard her! You hear? Do you *dare* to criticize *me*, Starbuck?'

In the face of that wrath, that roar, most men would have turned tail, but though Starbuck was trembling visibly, he held his ground, his face as red and screwed up as a man near the open door of a furnace.

'Not criticize, sir. Plead. Beg. Shouldst we not try to understand one another better, sir? In the interests of the owners? In the interests of this voyage of ours? If 'tis not to earn a living . . . if 'tis not to keep our wives and families in bread . . . exactly what . . . where exactly . . .' He searched about for words as carefully as David choosing stones for his slingshot in the shadow of Goliath. 'Into what darkness art thou hurrying us, sir?'

'Darkness? Not darkness, Starbuck! Into the whiteness, Starbuck, that's where!' Ahab, his face contorted with mania, snatched up a gun—a musket—and pointed it at his mate's chest.

We froze at our posts, cringed and buckled, heads down, knees bending. But Starbuck did not flinch, even though Ahab's finger was white on the trigger. 'Don't try and pit your God against me, Quaker! There's only one God on board this ship, and I'm it!' blared Ahab. 'On board the *Pequod*, I'm the One God, Father Almighty, Maker of Heaven and Earth, you hear?'

The small muscles of Starbuck's face twitched, but not with fear so much as outrage. He turned his back on the gun and walked, with dignity, to the head of the ladder, before turning back once more. 'Thy blasphemy appals me, sir. But I shall not say, "Beware of Starbuck". If I didst, thou wouldst laugh in my face. No. I tell you, "Beware of Ahab. Let Ahab beware of Ahab".'

'Huh!' scoffed Ahab, storming to the head of the ladder as though repelling enemy boarders. 'Too little a man to face me out, eh? Worm! Shrimp! Jumped up little fo'c'sle lawyer!'

But Starbuck had returned to the ship's prow, shoulders square, face set against the captain's quarterdeck and towards the open sea. Between the two men lay the main hold awash with precious whale oil, as the fruits of our year-long labours oozed slowly out into the bilges and away.

'Ahab beware of Ahab. Ahab beware of Ahab,' I heard the captain mutter repeatedly under his breath, while Pip ran and clasped his hand like an adoring child, and whimpered and worshipped:

'. . . One Lord, Father Almighty, Maker of Heaven and . . .'

At length, Ahab shook him off. He cupped his hand round his mouth and shouted up towards the mast-head:

'Furl the top-gallant and close-reeve the topsails fore and aft! Heave-to, men, then break open the main hold. Mr Starbuck informs me we have a leak of oil that must be attended to.'

Starbuck whirled round, his face alive with delight and gratitude. Mate and master looked at one another along the length of the ship; I do believe the mutual respect they felt, just then, for one another could have been the beginning of friendship.

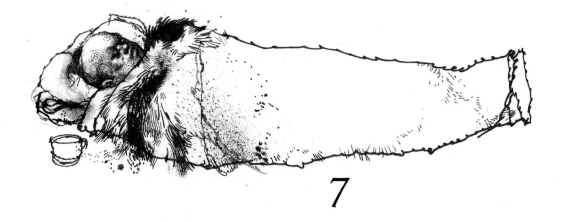

7

Queequeg's Canoe

WE sweated in that hold, like damned souls in Hell. We tipped barrels, rolled barrels, lifted barrels, hoopered and hammered and sealed barrels till the perspiration burst from our skins as though we too had sprung leaks. By the end of the day, I had the impression that the oil swilling about, ankle-deep, in the bilges, was not spilled oil at all, but our own sweat.

In fact, we shifted the barrels about, while Queequeg lifted them. Being mere Christian mortals, our strength had its limits. But Queequeg was a giant, a block-and-tackle of a man, a man with muscles like hawsers and a grip like grappling hooks. He heaved and hoisted and hauled the barrels up on to deck as if they were hay bales. Even so, his tattooed body ran so wet with sweat that some of the inks were loosened; they mingled in smudged clouds across his back and thighs. Dressed in nothing but a pair of woollen shorts, he was still so hot, in that confined, stinking pit, that he steamed whenever he emerged into the cold fresh air above.

When, at last, all the barrels had been checked for leaks and returned to the hold, Queequeg pulled himself out through the open hatch. He swayed for a moment on the brink of the hold, then toppled into a heap of tarpaulins, asleep before he even hit deck.

He should never have slept there like that, in only his shorts, his sweat dried by the cold night air. I should have covered him over, got him down to his own hammock, made sure he was all right. But I was so weary, it was all I could do to climb into my own hammock. In the morning, Queequeg was gibbering with cold. By afternoon, he was burning with fever. By nightfall, his life hung in the balance.

I could do nothing—only sit by him and reproach myself with not having taken better care of my friend. I sat beside him as helpless and useless as a blind look-out. When he stirred at around midnight, I helped him to a sip of water, and had the impression that shutters were closing behind his grey-brown eyes. 'Call carpenter,' was all he said.

The ship's carpenter sidled unwillingly up to my sick friend, superstitiously afraid to have his name spoken by a man so near to death. 'What's he want?' he asked me, avoiding a direct look into Queequeg's face.

Before I could answer, Queequeg whispered raspingly, 'When Queequeg dead . . .'

'No, Queequeg, no!' I protested.

'. . . when Queequeg dead, you not sling his hammock in sea, you hear?' He looked straight past me at the carpenter. 'No hammock. Make canoe for Queequeg. Canoe with lid.'

'A coffin, you mean?' The carpenter had never been commissioned to build a coffin by the man meant to lie in it.

When a man dies at sea, his body is sewn into his hammock and, like a butterfly unable to escape its chrysalis, is consigned to the bottomless cold. Not Queequeg. Queequeg wanted a different kind of funeral.

'You want a coffin?' the carpenter said again, and I thought for a moment that he was going to complain at the extra work, at the time it would cost him. 'A coffin. As you like.' He paced out the great length of my friend, banging his big boots heel-against-toe, heel-against-toe. 'Hmmm. Take a deal of wood.'

Queequeg trickled some coins into the carpenter's palm, then turned his face into the folds of his hammock. 'You make. Queequeg sleep now.'

With planks and nails, set-square and mallet, the chippy set to, building a coffin. He caulked the seams and attached rope handles. He planed it, oiled it and even worked a 'Q' on the lid with a chisel. When it was finished, Queequeg asked us to lift him into it.

'Harpoon!' he said, and we laid his beside him. 'Water!' and I set down a cup by his hand. 'Biscuits!' he said, and I ran and fetched them, laying them down his chest—one, two, three—like the buttons on a gingerbread man. I rolled up a piece of sailcloth, too, and placed it under his head.

'God!' said Queequeg, and the other men took one fearful step backwards. But I knew what Queequeg meant, and went to fetch the carved wooden idol to which he said his prayers, placing it between his hands. 'Now close hatch,' he said. 'Goodbye.'

We pulled the lid up to his chin like bedclothes. Then over his face. Beneath it, his voice said, '*Parmai*. It will do.' My friend had committed himself into the hands of his pagan gods. He awaited death inside his wooden canoe with all the regal dignity of King Arthur bound for Avalon.

And I was shut out, left behind in the world of the living. I did not argue, though. I did not hammer on the coffin lid or throw it aside. I am a sailor, too, and I was afraid of looking Death directly in the face. So I kept vigil nearby; a Christian man paying his last respects to a dead pagan— though all I could think of, in place of prayers, were all the thanks I had left unspoken, the favours I had never been able to repay. One hour passed, two hours, a third.

Then Queequeg opened up his coffin lid and climbed out again.

'*Queequeg! You're not dead!*'

'No. I remember. Something Queequeg not do.' He weighed his harpoon in his hands and made a few practice passes with it.

'D'you mean to say you remembered something you'd forgotten to do, so you decided not to die after all?'

'Die some other day. Soon enough.' He began to unpack his seaman's bag into the coffin, to use it as a sea-chest.

'Is that *possible?*' I gasped incredulously.

'Of course,' said Queequeg. 'Man want to die, nothing can save him. Man want to live, only God can kill him—or whale or storm, maybe.'

'It's a miracle!' I exclaimed, watching my friend wrap up his wooden god with infinite care and place it in one corner of the chest. But Queequeg simply shrugged and went on arranging his belongings— which left me wondering whether I had mistaken how sick he was, or if miracles came two-a-penny in Queequeg's universe.

Ahab had granted permission for the carpenter to expend time and wood making Queequeg a coffin. When Queequeg changed his mind about dying, and emerged on deck, after a day's rest, as fit as he had ever been, Ahab seemed deeply unsettled by it.

The *Pequod* had entered the Sea of Japan, and the pickings were rich. We killed four whales in a day. Three took all day to lash to the ship; the fourth had to be left floating at a distance from the *Pequod*. One little row-boat moored alongside it, till morning brought light enough to work by. I was among the crew of that little boat. So was Ahab.

Someone stuck an oar into the dead whale's spout-hole, and hung a lamp on top which cast a golden halo round both whale and boat. We dozed as best we could over our oars. Fedallah did not sleep, of course. The captain's fortune-teller simply crouched at the prow, head between his knees, gazing down at sharks attracted by the light and smell of death.

All of a sudden, Ahab set the boat rocking as he started up out of a shallow sleep. 'I dreamt it again!' he cried out.

The rowers stirred in their sleep. I opened my lashes a fraction, and listened, listened to the soothing purr of Fedallah's voice, his smiling, conspiratorial whispers. 'You dreamed of the hearse again?'

'Yes, yes! A funeral hearse with plumes, moving over the water towards me . . . Why should I dream hearses? Men who die at sea never lie in any hearse, do they? Do they?'

'And yet I tell you,' said the soothing voice, 'you shan't die until you have seen just such a sight.'

Ahab laughed an unsteady laugh. 'Then I'll die on dry land, and that's certain. Tell me again what you said about us, Fedallah, about you and me.'

'I said I would go ahead of you, captain, to be your pilot.' Fedallah's eyes glowed like fireflies in the lamplight. 'I've told you before. Only hemp rope can kill you, Ahab.'

'The gallows, you mean! A hangman's noose! I'm immortal, then! On this voyage, immortal!'

'I did not say . . .' Fedallah began.

But Ahab was peering down the boat, as if alerted to an eavesdropper among his sleeping crew. I quickly shut my eyes and pretended to be deep asleep. In fact I shut my eyes so tight that the veins in my eyelids presented strange patterns and distorted pictures: a hearse pulled over the waves by galloping horses plumed with black feathers, and bearing a sea-chest in place of a coffin . . .

So that was why Ahab kept Fedallah by him—his mascot, his talisman, his witchcraft. Fedallah's prophecies had convinced him that death would take Fedallah before ever it sank its teeth into Ahab. So, while Fedallah lived, Ahab felt no fear for his life, no fear from whale, water, or thunderbolt. That's no good thing. A man who thinks he cannot die, becomes reckless, forgets to fear God, forgets to preserve the lives of those around him.

Next day, Ahab stood at the quarterdeck rail, his quadrant raised to eye-level, taking his bearing from the sun. Charts lay around his feet like white shavings from his new ivory leg. All of a sudden, in a fit of impatient rage, he yelled, 'What good are you if you can't tell me where to look? Do you show me where Moby Dick's hiding himself? Useless lump of metal! Well, to the devil with you! I'll find my way by instinct from now on, as the whales do!' And he pitched the quadrant over into the water—a navigational instrument of precision-crafted brass chased with numbers, scales and curlicues and worth a whole fistful of money. Those who saw it go made an involuntary start towards the rail and looked back at the glassy water where it must have sunk, lost for ever.

I looked to Starbuck, as I always did to judge whether a thing mattered or not. (He was my quadrant, in a sort of way, I suppose, and always gave a true reading.) Starbuck's face was white. Without a ship knowing its exact bearing, its true position on the great gridded sea, how is she to know where she lies in relation to reefs, to whaling grounds, to a safe haven? How can a man interpret the coastlines he sees, or navigate

the starry mazes of the night sky? Only a madman throws his quadrant into the sea.

Ahab looked up and saw his crew staring open-mouthed, or hanging over the rail. 'It slipped from my hands,' he blarted out. But that did nothing to comfort the majority. To superstitious sailors such accidents are proof of bad luck looming.

'It's an omen! An evil omen!' they muttered to one another, as Ahab, unafraid of death, kicked a chart to tatters with his ivory peg.

8

Bad Omens

THE typhoon burst like a bomb. One moment the seas were a calm, ineffable blue, cradling the setting moon in tender swells; the next it was rending and tossing and thrashing itself into a liquid mountain range, a string of volcanoes spouting spray, a crumbling of sodden skies. The wind came out of the east — from the very compass mark at which Ahab was steering. It took off our canvas in one, two, three gusts, and left the intricate web of rigging howling and naked. It was as though the wind were trying to blow us back the way we had come — like when Odysseus opened the bag of captive winds and was driven back across an entire ocean. Shriller, less tuneful, than the sound of the wind in the rigging was the noise of Stubb singing.

'Must thou keep up that infernal row!' cried Starbuck at last, clutching Stubb by the shoulder. 'Could we not weather this storm in reverent silence?'

'You be brave quietly,' Stubb replied. 'Me, I'm not a brave man. I need to sing to keep my spirits up.' And on he sang, all melody lost amid the cacophony of wind, rain, and thunderclaps, a bawling, jolly tune about the joys of being at sea.

Ahab, hidden by darkness as he hauled himself along the ship's rail, suddenly leapt into plain sight, as three rivers of lightning poured simultaneously down the sky. His face was a picture of ecstasy, his mouth, agape for breath, overflowed with rainwater like a choked drain.

With a judder, as though the ship had foundered on solid rock, one of the lightning bolts struck the *Pequod*'s main mast, a hand's breadth above the gold dubloon of Ahab's bribe. The noise was ear-splitting, the light blinding. A visitation of angels all armed with blazing swords could hardly have struck more fear into a company of men.

I saw all my comrades, clear as day, frozen within a single illuminated second of their lives—twenty or so men clinging on to a flimsy heap of planks in the middle of the ocean. Every face was turned upwards—every face lit to a chalk-white. Then hands went up to shield each pair of eyes against the bright white light of fire.

The masts burned not with the crackling, jolly hearthside glow, but with a blue phosphorescence which did not char—an ice-blue dazzle that jabbed at the eyeball. The fire plumed from the masthead, crawled out along the spars, streamed like banners till the other two masts kindled with the same blue-white fire. Ahab lowered his hands from his eyes.

'Go on, then! Blind me!' he bellowed up at the mast. 'They call me Old Thunderer: so deafen me with your thunder! Scorch up my brains! Cut my head from my shoulders with your yellow fretsaw! All right, you're stronger than I—I know it! All right, you have the power of life and death! Thine is the honour, the power, and the glory! I know it! But I do know how to worship you! Love's no good! Fear's no good! Defiance, that's the only thing you understand! Well, I defy you! I'll defy you to my last breath!'

Who was he defying? God? The Devil? The storm? Or had Moby Dick, that nightmare obsession of his, grown into something elementally huge. 'Look up, men! Look up! This is the white fire that lights our way to the White Whale!'

'Dost thou not see, captain?' pleaded Starbuck. His feet were washed from under him by a wave breaking over the ship and rolling him along the deck. He looked like some Reformation white-plaster saint cast out-of-doors into the mud. 'Dost thou not see? God means you to turn back! How

many signs dost thou need, old man? Ten plagues, like Pharoah? God means you to turn back! Make for home, Captain Ahab. Heaven sets every obstacle in thy path! God mobs thee with angels' messengers—shows you omens past number! Look at thy boat, old man!'

He gestured wildly at the row-boat Ahab and the Filipinos used to hunt whale. A wave had stove in the bottom, like an empty eggshell holed with a spoon. A tongue of blue flame was flickering at the head of Ahab's harpoon where it stood in the prow: a phosphorescent serpent.

'The ship's log is gone—broken away . . . and the lifebuoy's lost overboard. The wind is set to blow us all back to Nantucket! Ride it, old man! God is against thee! Turn for home!'

We crew broke out of our trance and ran for the ropes: though there was not a scrap of sail left to raise, we went through the motions of putting about. Starbuck had to be right. God meant us to go home.

Ahab, hopping and striding recklessly along the streaming deck, reached the maimed row-boat, snatched up the harpoon with its halo of fire, and brandished it, the greatest savage of all, among a crew of warriors and braves. 'If one man makes a move to turn this ship about, so help me I'll put this through his chest and use him like whale-meat after! You swore to hunt the White Whale to the death, and to the death you're hunting him with me! *To the death, d'you hear?*'

The veiling rain extinguished the fire along the three masts, and inky blackness fell over the ship once more. On the afternoon when Jesus died, the sky must have turned that kind of black; the earth heaved in Jerusalem then, as the sea was heaving under us. Starbuck looked up at the three masts and saw three crosses against a lightless sky. This voyage had brought him to Golgotha, and he had done nothing—nothing, but stand by and watch his God's crucifixion.

What more could he have done? Seize control of the ship? After the storm, I was on watch in the yards and saw Starbuck's black-clad figure move swiftly down the length of the ship towards Ahab's cabin. I thought that something of the sort might be in his mind. That's why I followed on behind. That's why I watched and listened.

Starbuck hesitated in front of the door. It was unfastened and swung open and shut as the ship rolled, letting the light escape in periodic flashes, like a lighthouse beacon. Starbuck could see that Ahab sat dozing in his screwed-down chair. Beyond him, on the wall, a row of muskets stood in their rack, while another stood propped between Ahab's knees.

I saw Starbuck ease it out of Ahab's grasp and check to see if it was loaded. 'This is the gun you pointed at me,' he said under his breath. 'You were ready to use it, too, weren't you? Shoot me down like a dog.' He levelled the gun so that its barrel pointed directly at Ahab's chest.

'Is there no other way?' I heard him whisper. I flinched and snatched my hands into my pockets, thinking that he had seen me, wanted my permission to shoot. But, of course, Starbuck's conversation was with his conscience. A good angel at his right shoulder told him, '*No! What worse sin than murder?*' A tempter at his left shoulder retorted, '*Yes, and Ahab will murder every man on this ship if he is not stopped.*'

'I could make him a prisoner till the ship puts safely into port,' Starbuck argued and then, picturing it, shuddered from head to foot. The thought of shackling Ahab was as ridiculous as caging the Medusa: those eyes, once open, would turn every man aboard to stone; his bullying would get him free before the ship had gone forty leagues. No, the only

realistic way was to fell him in his tracks, like a charging elephant, to finish him before he woke, to spill him before he spilled every life on the *Pequod* in his quest for revenge. Starbuck's finger whitened on the trigger.

The words were in my mouth: 'Do it! Kill him! Shoot!' But they tasted vile, and my cheeks, too, sweated with horror. I also wanted to say, 'Don't do it, Starbuck! Think of your soul, Starbuck!'

For once, Starbuck was not thinking of his soul, but of his greatest joy, his family. 'One shot and I'll live to see you again, Mary. One shot and I come home to you, son, my own little boy. Let him live and he'll drown me thousands of miles from you, in some ocean so deep I'll be sinking day after day to my resting place, and never be found. Not ever found. One more shipwrecked sailor never going home. One more fatherless home. Oh, God, help me? Shall I? Must I? Is that what you want, Lord? Where are you? Great God, *where?*'

77

Old Testament Jacob, wrestling with God himself, never struggled as hard as Starbuck at the door of Ahab's cabin. A sign. One single signal would have given him the courage to shoot. But no sign came.

No god spoke to Starbuck, and little by little, the great hypnotic power of Ahab's personality worked its spell. Even sleeping, his larger-than-life willpower overwhelmed Starbuck, like a man on a beach, cut off by a tide. He laid the musket on Ahab's lap again, turned suddenly on his heel—and caught sight of me in the swinging lamplight. In my horrified fascination, I had forgotten to hide myself.

Starbuck made no explanation—no garbled excuses. He simply said, 'I came to tell him the wind is gone about. It stands perfect for his purposes. Perfect for his evil, godless purposes . . . But he's too sound asleep to hear me. So I'd best rig the ship myself.'

He trimmed the ship to run due east, exactly as Ahab wished, exactly in accordance with Ahab's conviction that there, somewhere along that invisible blue line, lay a predestined rendezvous with Moby Dick.

The ship turned, but the compass-needle did not. The lightning strike had demagnetized the metal, and it swung to and fro without the smallest interest in magnetic north. Yet another stroke of bad luck, you might say. Yet another evil omen, said the crew of the *Pequod*. Yet another effort by God's angels, thought Starbuck, to deflect Ahab from his sinful self-destruction. But Ahab still had the sun to steer by, and until the angels plucked that off the sky, he would go on sailing due east, revenge filling his patched and tattered sails.

It was a terrible sound that woke us next day. At first Stubb tried singing, to drown it out, but both his voice and his humour failed him. We were sailing past a cluster of rocky islets when the noise came to us on the wind. It was a noise like a child crying.

'Mary, see to the boy!' cried Starbuck, waking in his hammock.

The single cry became two, five, twenty sobbing cries. Bethlehem must have sounded like that the night Herod sent his soldiers to kill all the newborn boys.

'*Mermaids!*' said Stubb.

'No,' said Manxman, and since he was the oldest man aboard and must have learned more than most about the sea, we looked towards him expectantly. 'It's the souls of sailors newly drowned. In that last storm, I dare say,' said Manxman, and I felt my soul shudder within me and clutch for a tighter hold on my body.

'No, no! It's Pip, that's who! It's Pip wanting to come aboard, but you mustn't let him!' I looked around for whose shrill piping voice had said it, and saw Pip himself, limp-legged with fright, clinging to the rail and pointing, pointing out to sea. 'Look, it's Pip all right! I see his black hands reaching out the water! Don't let that coward back aboard! You won't, will you? Don't!'

Ahab came on deck at the sound of Pip's hysterical caterwauling. He went straight to the boy and soothed him, stroking his woolly hair and speaking to him in a voice as soft as a mother's. 'Come down to my cabin, child. Calm yourself.'

'It's Pip, sir! It's Pip out there! That wicked coward what jumped, sir, when he was told never to jump, sir. Don't let him on board, sir! This ship don't need no cowards, sir!'

'There, there, boy. You're safe with me . . . though your name quite slips my mind. What should I call you?'

'Bell-boy, sir! I ring the ship's bell, sir!'

'Well then, Bell-boy, don't be afraid. I'll not leave you alone till you're easier in your mind.'

We stared at him—the bestial Ahab soothing a frightened lunatic, while the magic sea all around us rang with dreadful cries.

'Mermaids, sir!' said Stubb pointing towards the rocks and the noise.

'The souls of dead sailors,' said Manxman darkly.

'Seals,' snarled Ahab. 'Did you never hear seal pups cry in the sealing season? Pah! You're more of a halfwit than this one here!' and he led Pip tenderly back to his cabin, blaming Manxman for upsetting the child with nonsense. As he passed his first mate in the companionway, he thrust Pip at Starbuck as if he were producing a piece of damning evidence in court. 'And you really think your God's a caring God? A loving God? A God who does this to a child, then turns his back? A God who can burden an innocent soul with something as terrible as *madness?*'

Either Starbuck did not have a ready answer, or Ahab did not stay to hear it.

'There go two as mad as each other!' muttered Manxman crudely. 'One's mad with weakness, t'other's mad with power . . . And I still say that's the souls of drowned sailors crying out to us.'

I partly believe he was right.

9

Unhappy *Rachel*

'Have you seen the White Whale?'
'Yesterday! Have you seen a whale-boat adrift?'

CHOKING down his joy, Ahab cried out for a boat to take him aboard the ship *Rachel*, as she drew alongside. But it seemed that the *Rachel's* captain was in an even greater hurry to speak with Ahab, for he fairly tumbled into a boat and crossed to the *Pequod* breathless with haste. The two men knew each other. They were both Nantucket captains.

Ahab hauled him aboard, eyes blazing and with an exultant grin, missing out all the formal greetings so as to heap questions on the man's head. 'Where did you see the whale? Yesterday, you say? You didn't kill him? He's not dead, is he? Which direction?'

Captain Gardiner wore a strange expression such as I've seen on Newfoundlandmen, their faces frozen with cold till the muscles cease to function. He barely parted his lips when he spoke, nor blinked his eyes, nor removed his hands from his pockets, but looked back at Ahab with a gaze every shred as wild. Did the White Whale have this effect on men?

'I had three boats out already, hunting a pack of whales,' Gardiner recounted. 'Suddenly, up rears this white monster, and I shout for the fourth boat—the spare—to go after it. The harpoon made a good fix, but the white whale up and ran, towing the boat behind it. That's nothing, though, is it? It happens. Boats get towed. Either the whale tires or the boat cuts loose. No great matter. Not if you can find the boat again. I had to wait to pick up the first three teams, so it was sunset by the time I could start looking. I've searched all night and all this morning.'

81

Beside me, Queequeg said, 'Was something in that boat. Something he want back bad.'

'His best boat, maybe,' said Manxman.

'His best harpooner,' suggested Flask.

'You'll help, won't you?' Gardiner was saying to Ahab. 'The two of us—if we worked together—we'll find them far quicker. You'll help. I'll charter your ship—pay for your time! You won't be out of pocket, I promise you! But you'll join in the search, won't you. You must.'

'Oh, Christ. It's his son,' said Starbuck, with a flash of insight. 'The man's son is lost in that boat.'

'My only boy—my son,' said Captain Gardiner, his hard-rimmed mouth buckling. 'He was in that fourth boat. Twelve years old—his first voyage. He's out there somewhere, drifting. But together we could find him in no time! The two of us . . . if we're systematic . . .'

We must find him, I thought.

'He's not drifting, he's drowned,' whispered Manxman. 'We heard his soul crying out yesterday, remember?' But he would never have said as much to the desperate Captain Gardiner. The news of a son dying is too much for any man to accept; he needs proof. We would help him look. We had to help him look. All the codes of the sea bound us to help him look.

But Ahab said nothing, simply stood and reddened his cheek with rubbing ferociously at the white stubble of his beard.

'I won't go till you say yes!' said Gardiner, with an attempt at cheeriness which crumbled into terror. 'I'd do the same for you, God knows, if it were your boy. And you do have a boy, don't you, Ahab?'

There was a stir among the crew of the *Pequod*. Ahab, a child? Ahab, a little son? To us he was an old man—a cripple—a man with nothing in his heart but a hatred for whales. Now we had to think of him as a man like Starbuck, with a wife and child at home.

'No. I can't do it,' said Ahab, and we reeled once more with disbelief. 'Even now I'm losing time talking to you. I'm very sorry about your . . . misfortune, but I have business to attend to.' Then, turning his back on Gardiner, he spoke sharply to Starbuck: 'See that all strangers are off this ship in three minutes, first mate, then set the same course as before.'

With a writhe of the hips to uproot his ivory stump, he limped below decks to his cabin, leaving Captain Gardiner transfixed to the spot. He looked at us—resting those desolate, pleading eyes on each man in turn. And all we could think to do for this soul in torment was to turn our backs on him as well, and man our posts. We were under the command of the devil himself, it seemed, and powerless to do any decent deed of humanity.

82

Without a word more, Gardiner returned to his ship, and soon the *Pequod* and the *Rachel* struck off on different courses and parted, leaving their wakes tangled in the one spot, like the tails of sea serpents. The *Rachel* crossed the swell, and spray broke over her bows so that she wept salt tears from bowsprit and prow as she went back to her solitary, sorrowful search.

We had sailed into the selfsame sea where Ahab lost his leg to Moby Dick. After the meeting with the *Rachel*, he confined Pip to his cabin — 'You may sit in my chair, boy, and listen out for my steps coming and going, but I can't keep you by me any more' — and never went down there again. Day and night he kept to the quarterdeck, propped in a standing position, with a waterproof hat pulled low over his face. It was impossible to tell when his eyes were open or shut, so that every man aboard felt watched continually, obliged to carry out his duties unthinkingly.

Every half-hour the ship's bell rang, and every half-hour Ahab bellowed up at his look-outs, 'What d'you see?'

'Nothing!' came the reply. Every half-hour for three days.

At last, exasperated to the point of disbelieving his own look-outs, Ahab rigged himself a bo'sun's chair and had us winch him up into the shrouds. 'I'll sight him myself,' he snarled. 'I'll keep that gold dubloon myself, you blind puppies, you purblind moles!'

We crowded the yard-arms like blossoms along the boughs of a tree, and overhead swung Ahab — a black thundercloud hovering over his own ship, or a pirate hung up in tar and chains to be an example to others. We did not cut through the ropes. We did not let him plummet to the deck and die of a broken neck. We obeyed like machinery men, and there was no joy or misery in us — only the burning certainty that something was about to happen.

A black sea-hawk with a beak red as blood came flapping out of the sky's attics and lazily circled the tallest mast, dropping lower and lower in

its curiosity. Ahab barely noticed it, so hard was he scanning the sea. The bird rose up high, then fluttered down again around Ahab's head, as flies in the desert pester a man. Then, all of a sudden, the bird lifted the hat from Ahab's head and flew with it out to sea—on and on, carrying its prize. Only at the very brim of the horizon did the hawk let the hat fall—a black full-stop dropping slowly, slowly on to a paper ocean.

It was a beautiful day, the sea a multitude of jewelled colours, tessellated light, tasselled waves, and a breeze like a silk banner. The beauty Ahab saw from his dizzy roost must have touched some part of his soul which Boomer nor Gardiner nor Starbuck nor God had been able to touch till now. A single tear rolled down the scar-groove in his face, and fell through space as his hat had done. It fell on Starbuck, balanced on the yard-arm below—splashed on to his face like the first drop of a shower. The first mate looked up at the sound of his name.

'Oh, Starbuck!' sighed Ahab. 'My first day at sea was a day like this. Forty years ago now. When I think of the life I've led since then! The work, the weariness; hunger and thirst; hot and cold . . . I married my wife between voyages—set sail the day after my wedding and was gone three years. What kind of marriage is that? What manner of an earthquake life . . . half dead with fright or half drowned with boredom. Killing whales. What a forty-year fool I've been to live a life like that . . . Do I look as old as I feel, Starbuck? I feel as if I've been crawling over the ocean since Adam quit Paradise, the centuries piling up on my back . . . Oh, Starbuck, what it is to be so intolerably old!'

The words showered down on Starbuck, and, in drenching him, filtered down to me swinging in the lower rigging like a spider on a dewy web. 'About now, my boy will be waking up after his midday nap,' said Ahab. 'He'll be sitting up—laughing. My wife will be telling him again how I'm off over the deep blue sea and coming back soon to dance with him . . .'

'Just like my Mary!' gasped Starbuck as if it were barely credible there could be two such households in the world. 'Every day she carries my boy to the top of the hill behind our house—to watch out for Daddy coming home. Oh, God! Let's go home to them, Ahab! For God's sake, let's go home and see our boys waving to us from the hilltop!'

I touched the mast from which the shrouds were strung, and it seemed to be trembling, trembling with the shudders that shook Ahab to the core.

'*What is it that drives me on?*' he asked of the open sea. 'Against my better nature. Against all my natural longings and lovings? Why must I keep pushing on, pushing on, daring myself to do what I do? Is it me? Is it my doing? Or is it God's? Is it the way he made me? Is it the fate God's sewn into me? God made me! What does that make God? If I am as I am—what does that make God, eh? Isn't God the one to blame for making murderers and despots and madmen and . . . Starbuck!'

The first mate was lowering himself hand-over-hand out of the rigging. His hopes had been raised only to be dashed again; his face was a picture of despair. At the sound of his name, he did look up once more—and saw Ahab sniffing like a dog.

Fedallah, the skeleton-thin creature standing on the very yard-arm's end, leaned out even further over the ocean and also snuffed the air.

'I smell him, Starbuck!' breathed Ahab. 'I smell Moby Dick! I smell the barnacles on his back, the birds over him; I smell his sperm and his breath spouting. He's near, Starbuck! He's very, very near!'

85

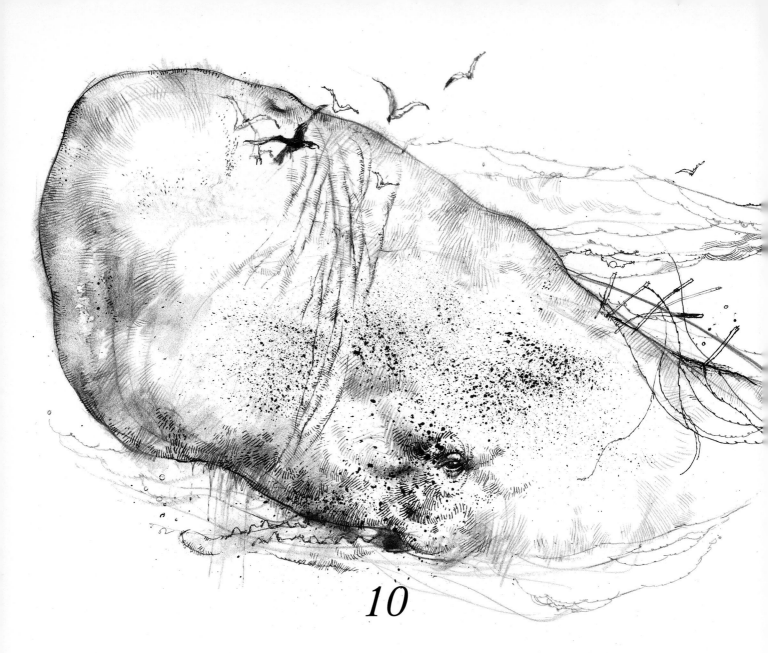

10

Moby Dick

'There she blows! Hump like a hill of snow! It's Moby Dick!'

SURE enough, he had seen it himself. No one else's heart was permitted to thrill at owning the gold dubloon: Ahab sighted Moby Dick before any other man, and his face shone gold in the low morning light.

'Lower three boats! Mr Starbuck, you stay aboard the *Pequod*. For the sake of that wife and son of yours. That's an order. Boats! *Boats!*'

When the whale rose a second time, we were close enough to see every furrow on its forehead, every tear in the flukes, every mangled and twisted harpoon grown home into its milk-white hide; the crooked jaw and the creamy bubbles cast up in its green wake. A whole society of birds flocked above the hump—black sea-hawks with blood-red beaks. As the whale dived once more, the birds wheeled away in a dozen directions and waited, many storeys of sky higher, for their island to reappear.

Of course, it was Ahab's crack crew of Filipinos which swung into action first, but Ahab himself was the harpooner in the prow of their boat. But after the rush to launch, we were all obliged to sit on a still sea for an hour, the white whale submerged so far beneath us that he might have been a dream and gone for ever.

Then Tashtego pointed up into the sky. 'The birds!' he cried, and we saw that from their watchtower, the hawks had seen their whale rising.

We looked over the side. No bigger than a white winter weasel, a shape was coming up from a depth of ocean no living man has ever seen. With every fraction of a second it doubled in size—a pebble, a bullet, a snowball, a cannon-ball, a meteorite—until it filled our sight entirely and made all the undersea white.

It rose under Ahab's boat—directly underneath it. The crooked jaw opened: even from my boat I could see the long twin rows of teeth shredding blue water into white bubbles, turning the sea to sour cream. Then Moby Dick closed his jaws around the Filipino boat. The crew threw themselves into the stern, spilling out over the transom as the boat was lifted entirely out of the water, in the jaws of Moby Dick.

Only Ahab was left in the prow when those crooked jaws bit the boat in two. The harpoon was jarred from his hand, and he reeled on his untrustworthy legs, cursing Moby Dick in language as foul as hot tar. Robbed of the power to wound or kill, he laid both hands on that jutting lower jaw, as if he would wrestle bodily with the spermaceti. But he lost his footing, the jaw was wet and glassy smooth. Ahab was thrown on his back, and it was all he could do to cling on, a hand over each gunwale and his face towards the sky. The two halves of the boat fell back into the sea, floating on the tilt, their smashed planks pointing at the sky.

Then the whale began to swim. He swam with a seemingly arrogant contempt, describing a circle in the sea, holding prisoner the stricken row-boat: it kept us other boats from moving any closer. Indeed, we rowed for our lives in the opposite direction. I thought that at any moment Moby Dick would break away to snap at a second boat. But his small black eye was fixed on the splintered wreckage, and its flukes drove it faster and faster, round the scene of triumph. A vortex began to spin—a revolving circle of trapped water dipping lower and lower in its centre—a whirlpool with Ahab at its centre. Moby Dick was toying with his prey.

Sun glinted on the corkscrew forest of broken harpoons embedded in its hump, and on the iceberg mass of its gliding body. Its crooked jaw impersonated a grin of malicious pleasure, while its wrinkled brow scowled. The sea-hawks overhead shrieked with glee.

'*Steer for the whale!*' Ahab's voice was snatched away by the loud hissing of foam and screech of birds. He was floundering, helpless, clinging to his spinning cockleshell of a half-boat, his ivory leg sticking out from it as vulnerable as a match. With every other spin of the revolving boat, he tried to pull his head over the gunwale so that Starbuck, aboard the *Pequod*, might see him, hear his bellow, read the command off his face.

He must have managed this at last, for with a crack of sails unfurling,

the *Pequod* changed course, heeling over and turning till its bone bowsprit pointed directly at Moby Dick like an accusing finger. On came the mother-ship, equal in size to the great white whale, and gathering momentum out of a spanking wind. She bore down on the circling whale: collision was certain unless the beast broke off from its sport. We in the little boats held our breath.

Just when it seemed the *Pequod* would strike the iceberg whale and that both would be stove in, Moby Dick sank out of sight. With flailing of flukes high as the masthead, he was away — away, away in a line as straight as a Roman road across the pathless sea.

The whirlpool slowed and grew shallow. The two sections of broken whaler spun in the eddy, then capsized and sank. We picked the swimmers up from a calm sea strewn with broken oars and bench slats.

The Filipino hands were gibbering and hysterical. But Fedallah their leader spoke not a word. He simply squatted on the foredeck, his head between his bony knees, and stared out to sea. Ahab, fired with a kind of ecstasy, limped to the main mast and the gold dubloon.

'This is mine by rights!' he said. 'I saw him first. By rights this is mine. But I'll let it hang there for now. I'll still give it to the man who sights Moby Dick on the day we kill him. Not long now, boys! Not long now!'

Starbuck exploded with frustration. 'Was this not warning enough to thee, man? What plainer omen could the angels shake at thee than this . . . this . . . *nightmare?* Thy own sweet life snatched out of the mouth of that lime-dust monster? Be told! Give thanks thou wert spared, man! And don't go after Moby Dick a third time!'

Ahab looked out from under the brim of his borrowed hat — the look of a Faustus who has bought a guarantee of life from the Devil and knows he cannot die. 'D'you really think that's the way the gods would speak to men if they had something to say? Do you? In omens? A nudge and a hint, like some whispering fishwife on the dock-quay? Do you? If God's got something to say to me, let him spit it out in plain words! Till then, I've got unfinished business with that white fiend out there. Get to your post, Mr Starbuck, and keep a sharp watch for Moby Dick! We'll dog him till he's dead with my harpoon in his eye!'

Through day and into night, through night and into day, we went in pursuit of Moby Dick, striking off along the course he had taken after the first encounter. Every shred of sailcloth was hauled up: the *Pequod* bounded over the sea at a glorious, reckless speed, the hull thrumming with the rush of water around it, the rigging singing with wind. Our hair streamed behind us with the sheer momentum. Our hearts beat faster, because of the vibrations of the deck. Surely we would outrun the whale, making such speed?

But no.

'*The White Whale! He breaches!*' Rather than glide smoothly into view and loose a lazy fountain of sparkling breath, Moby Dick breached, as only a sperm whale can. He erupted vertically, till his flukes were all but clear of the water, before flopping down full-length. The splash was like an arsenal of gunpowder exploding, visible seven miles away. It made the diaphragm of the sea quake. It made the heart expand and contract. It made Ahab crow like a rooster.

Three boats sped outwards from the *Pequod*. They closed on Moby Dick from three sides. It was to be his death: Ahab's obsession would not outlive the day. The harpooners rained harpoons on him—two, three, four!—from each of the boats. Some sheered off, some made superficial wounds, but soon a web of ropes had been pinned to the beast's hump, and held him in the centre of a web.

Only then did he start to run, weaving between the row-boats, up and down, round and fro, until the ropes were a cat's-cradle confusion of loops and knots. The boats were being pulled in closer and closer to the whale's body. Then he swam directly into the mesh of ropes, jaws gaping and snagging and snatching.

Flask's boat and mine were dragged together and smashed, side against side, with a splintering of wood. We spilled into the water, yelling till the fear filled our mouths, terrified of our own ropes now, for fear *we* become entangled in them and drown.

I swam oh-so-calmly—no splashing out for the nearest piece of flotsam, no thrashing of legs to get away from the scene. These were shark-infested waters, and every man drew up his legs and tried to be invisible to the roaming packs which might even now be converging on the disturbance. We spread our arms on the water, we looked about us for

Moby Dick, but we held very still, faces deadpan with fear, waiting in the water for death or rescue.

The great white whale had gone, disappeared, like the ghost it resembled. It had gone deep. And yet how deep could it go? Stuck with harpoons, trailing ropes and wreckage, how deep could Moby Dick dive? It was not long before we found out.

Up he came once more, breaching directly beneath Ahab's boat—a stone white monolith standing on the sea's wave with a row-boat smashed across its apex, and men falling like pieces of moss.

Perhaps he stunned himself with his own violence, but Moby Dick lay at a distance on his side regarding through one black eye the havoc he had wrought. Every time a fragment of boat, an oar, a plank touched his flank, his flukes thrashed with a drenching explosion of spray and debris. Then he swam calmly away, his crooked jaw grinning, the harpoon ropes trailing from his hump like a woman's long hair.

I was among the first to be picked up. I could not think but that half the ship's complement had died, and I began to search out friends. Queequeg! Where was Queequeg? He was alive. Stubb! Where was Stubb? He was unharmed. Flask! Where was Flask—and Tashtego and Tahiti? They had all been rescued, all spared by the tiger sharks and the vengeful whale. Where was Ahab?

We first knew he was alive when Starbuck helped him up over the side. The two men stood side by side, Ahab's arm round the first mate's neck, dragging his head down low. Starbuck could not withdraw his arm from round Ahab's waist, for the captain's ivory leg had been smashed off at the knee. Only a few jagged splinters of bone protruded below his coat.

'I worked hard on that leg, too,' said the carpenter, under his breath.

'Give me that harpoon for a stick,' said Ahab, and though his face was ashen with pain, he propped himself up with the harpoon crutch and swung himself along, making for his hoistable chair. 'Keep a sharp look-out, men,' he said, almost as if the fight with Moby Dick had been the merest upset in a well-ordered day. 'Whose will that dubloon be, boys, eh? Today's the second day. On the third day he'll rise again. And that's the day he'll die. It's written on my heart and conscience. That's the day he'll die. Who'll be the one to spy him first tomorrow, eh?'

Suddenly he looked round him, reckoning up the numbers of men assembled on the sun-bleached deck. 'Where's Fedallah?' he demanded.

We looked from face to face though, through sheer exhaustion, no one stirred from the spot where we stood steaming. *'Find him!'* cried Ahab in a parrot-screech of pure terror. 'Look below! Put out a boat! Look everywhere, but *find him!*'

Fedallah was not to be found. 'Must've got tangled in the ropes and towed under,' Stubb concluded, unable to counterfeit either shock or sorrow. Of all the men who might have died that day, Fedallah would be the least missed. I don't believe even his own boat crew felt grief at his loss.

Ahab, however, was inconsolable. He raged against the whale which had drowned his skeletal, smileless, ungodly prophet. He could spare quadrant, compass, and ship's log, it seemed, but not his soul's astrologer.

I thought back to the night spent moored beside the dead whale, and realized why. '*In the end, I will go ahead of you, to be your pilot,*' Fedallah had told Ahab. And now he had gone — gone ahead into the tangled wake of the white whale. The traitor had gone over to the enemy, and walked now in the train and livery of Moby Dick.

11

On the Third Day he Rises

THE sea that day was a summerhouse for angels, the weather sublime, the waves a roof of lapis lazuli over a mermaid palace, the sunlight beaten out to the thinness of gold leaf. There has never been a more beautiful day in all my life . . . nor a more terrible.

The *Pequod* leapt over the water; we seemed to be riding the wind towards the edge of the spinning world.

'On the third day he rises!' Ahab hallooed from his mast-top cradle, and all I could think, in this paradise of turquoise and scudding clouds, was that Christ rose on the third day and not the Devil.

Of Moby Dick, however, there was no sign. Though Ahab searched the sea with the unblinking eye of a ravenous gull, there was no whale. Misgivings worked him into a frenzy. Suddenly, at around noon, he realized his mistake. 'The ropes have slowed him down!' he declared, laughing, and spreading wide his arms and big hands, explaining to us, like a parent to young children. 'The tackle he's towing has slowed him down! We've overshot him in the night!'

Forty years had taught Ahab to think like a whale, to live in a whale's skull and cross oceans in the manner and wake of whales. If he had known less about whales, we might have left Moby Dick far behind us and never seen him again. But, of course, we turned about and retraced our morning's course. 'See how he hastes toward the open jaws,' muttered Starbuck, no longer caring whether he was overheard or not.

Aloft, Ahab's grim delight had returned. He felt immortal once more, enthroned in his crow's-nest chair, surveying the ocean as though he alone owned it.

Time held its breath. Every member of the crew hung in the rigging like flies in Ahab's web. *'There!'* Ahab's voice roared out, and soon every other starboard look-out was shouting. Far out at sea, a slab of white like an iceberg rose out of the sea.

Starbuck looked up at the cry of the look-outs. I saw his dark eyes shine. 'My hill? Can'st thou see my hill? And Mary, too? Is she holding the boy? Is my boy waving?' Then the daydream dissolved away and left on Starbuck's face nothing but dread.

My legs felt weak with fear, but somehow the rest of me was full of fire—the fire of anticipation making my heart pulse and shudder. Just as

Starbuck had fixed his thoughts entirely on wife and child, Ahab could see no one and nothing other than Moby Dick. Forehead to forehead they were about to collide. As we lowered him out of the rigging, he was already in conversation with it, that white demon of his, that tormentor.

'From the very first day of the world, we were destined to meet, you and I! Noah, when he looked out and saw the only whale in the world swim by—that was me looking out and seeing you! This battle of ours was fixed from the beginning of time . . . and now your time's come, Moby Dick!'

As his one foot touched the deck, he stumbled, and Starbuck caught him. 'The third day, Starbuck! The boat's under your command till I return from killing the white whale!' Their eyes met, their hands clasped.

'Oh, captain, don't go!'

'There now, Starbuck. Some men die on an ebb-tide, and some go on the flood. I'm an old man, Starbuck. Shake hands and let's part friends.'

'Oh, my captain! I—' Starbuck wept, and still their hands were joined.

I turned and embraced my friend Queequeg. I was bound for the boat, and he confined to the mothership by the shortage of boats. Ahab was to be the only harpooner aboard.

'Lower away!' grunted Ahab, and the whaler—the only undamaged row-boat left—dropped down the flank of the *Pequod*. I was in that boat.

As we passed the porthole of Ahab's cabin, Pip's black face bulging at eyes and cheeks looked out. 'Oh, master! The sharks! Don't go! Don't leave me! Don't go out among the sharks!'

There were sharks, too. They snapped at our oar tips as we rowed. The waves banged irritably on the boat's sides rap-rap-rapping for attention, but Ahab paid them none. Only hemp rope could kill Ahab—Fedallah had prophesied as much—not shark, nor drowning nor a mutinous bullet from his oh-so-silent crew.

What a silence we kept that day, waiting, waiting for Moby Dick to breach again.

At long last, the water round the boat bloated in a convex circle, as though the sea was coming to the boil. A low rumbling came from far below us. Then Moby Dick breached.

He came out of the ocean obliquely, like a missile propelled from a weapon of war. He was a great slab of marble shrouded in rainbows of spray, beautiful with rainbow ribbons but festooned with rope, tackle, and broken ironmongery, too. He swam past the boat, flailing his tail and buffeting it amidships. One side was smashed in, and we men dived to our knees, with harpoons for hammers, trying to knock the broken planks

back into place. The whale rolled past us—a juggernaut stone idol bearing down on its suicidal worshippers. It was then that Ahab glimpsed his pilot, his escort, his guide for the long voyage ahead. Fedallah had not deserted him at all. He had come back, as promised. Lashed to the flank of the whale by a dozen coils of harpoon rope, his dead eyes wide open, his body spread-eagled against a wall of whale-flesh, Fedallah rode the white whale. Only his forearm hung free of the tangling ropes and, as the whale dipped through the water, the prophet's hand rose and fell, beckoning. He passed within a metre of Ahab's face, water pouring from his open mouth like prophecies. We rose to our feet, like men on dry land who can turn and run from something too terrible to face.

'*Sit down!* Every man of you!' Ahab brandished his harpoon at us. 'If any living thing goes over the side of this boat, I swear I'll harpoon it in the water! So row, damn you! *Row!*'

When we pulled on our oars, the blades chewed the water as feebly as dinner forks. The tiger sharks had bitten the blades almost to the quick and we were rowing with poles, with sticks, with fingerposts.

Still, we need not have taxed ourselves; the whale came to us, not we to him. Its mouth open like the door of a marble vault, it came back to run its black eye over Ahab.

'The hearse! The hearse!' I heard him say, seeing his recurrent nightmare put on flesh and substance and swim towards him, mouth agape. But Fedallah's dead head rocked on its shoulders. Here was a vault, not a hearse. Fedallah went on beckoning, and his mouth went on spilling watery words, '*Come over, come over! Come over to the side of the Dead!*'

Ahab pulled himself to his feet, jamming his knee against the boat's side, bracing himself against the stempost. 'Give me all the spears!' he hissed, as if the whale might hear and understand him.

Why the whale, with all its weight of wisdom, waited there, I cannot guess. It is only a dumb brute, I told myself, but even then I did not believe it. Moby Dick lay in the ocean as white and furrowed as a brain scooped from its skull, a brain vast enough for God. So was this God who had risen on the third day all brain, all intellect, all cunning, all vengeance?

Ahab had us row so close that the breath from Moby Dick's blowhole shrouded us in fog-white mist. I could see nothing, my eyelids beaten shut by the spray, my nostrils full of the rank stench of whale. I could not see, but I knew that if I reached out a hand through that mist, the whale was so close my fingers would brush his barnacled hide.

Ahab threw one harpoon. The whale shuddered. The sea shuddered around the whale, the boat vibrated with that shudder as though it, too, had received a death wound. Moby Dick gave a writhe of rage. His flukes smashed against the boat like a hammer against an eggshell and I somersaulted upwards, backwards, far off the stern of the speeding boat.

The row-boat was using sail as well as oars: the sails were bellied out, full of wind. The boat sped away from me with no hope of my catching her up or even being heard crying for help, above the din of the spouting whale. I thought 'sharks!', and yet I watched and went on watching, spellbound. Like a man in the stalls of a theatre, I watched the drama of the whale acted out in front of me: a play, an entertainment, a puppet show for me alone. Those little souls, that massive whale against a backdrop of the mothership.

The harpoon wound was deep. Though the rope ran foul and had to be cut, the harpoon had injured the whale. It turned its face away, as though the offence done it was too great to bear, and sank out of sight.

Ahab clutched the prow and peered down into the water, but the rest of the men were in a frenzy to keep the boat afloat, baling water, shoving all manner of packing into the gaping hole in the base—coats, sailcloth, bits of plank, coils of rope. Ahab was looking so intently into the ocean's basement that it was Tahiti who saw Moby Dick returning.

'The ship! The ship!' he cried.

The whale had cruised in a circle to the far side of the *Pequod*. With reasoning worthy only of Man, he was himself bent on an act of deliberate revenge. He was going to sink the mothership.

'*Row! Row till your brains burst!*' screamed Ahab. '*Save my ship, won't you?*' Here was the wooded hearse of his nightmare: his own ship was the hearse he had dreamed.

And so the holed row-boat hurried, as best it could, back towards the *Pequod*, while, from the opposite side, a gigantic white whale charged. Lifting his head in an awkward, ungainly posture, and sawing it from side to side, he cut the water with his lower jaw, slopping sea into his gullet.

I saw Queequeg at the masthead, nailing a new flag to the jack. I saw him follow the progress of the whale from his high look-out, realize the whale's intention, and call out to the men below. I saw the men run to the ship's rail, then scatter from it, as the worst of places to be. Strangely calm, Queequeg turned and continued hammering, the flag wrapping itself around him like a shroud but his arm still hammering, hammering.

Moby Dick struck the *Pequod* below the waterline, and there was a noise of mountain cataracts, as the sea surged into the bowels of the ship. A silence followed, as the water found its own level through the *Pequod* and the whale lay still. Even the waves turned over more quietly, and I could plainly hear the sound of Queequeg's hammer and the voice of Starbuck: 'This is thy doing, Ahab. Now God stand by me!'

Bildad was running up and down the deck, his moneybag clutched to his chest. I saw the sun glint on Daggoo's ear-rings. Stubb was flinging off his boots and coat—anything that would pull a man under who fell into the sea. 'I see you grinning at me, whale!' he bellowed, with a laugh fit to break his heart. 'Let Stubb die in his drawers, if need be—I'm not proud!'

Moby Dick swam clear under the holed keel and up again, into the narrow space between *Pequod* and whale-boat. Once again it lay inert, doing nothing, as if to watch, with that keen, black eye and grinning jaw, how Ahab took his loss.

Indeed, Ahab held every eye. Standing up in the prow of the listing boat, like a preacher in a pulpit, weathered and scarred but head up and defiant, he harangued the whale. 'The *Pequod* goes down unconquered, whale! D'you see? Not a mast broke! Glorious ship, must we really die apart from each other? A ship without a captain and a captain without his ship: that's the saddest . . . Ah well. Lonely death after a lonely life, that's all it signifies. All right. All right. I'll turn my body from the sun.'

But Ahab did not sound submissive—not in the least. Rage was bubbling up within him just as the sea was bubbling into his row-boat and into his great, broken ship. He weighed a harpoon in the palm of his hand, and his lips drew back from his teeth, his lids from the passion in his eyes.

'I'm coming for you, Moby Dick. You may destroy me, but you'll never conquer me! You've pitched me down to Hell, monster, but even from Hell I can still reach up to stab you! For hate's sake, I spit my last breath at you! *Here's* how I surrender my spear to you!'

His harpoon flew with such force that it sank into the whale like a bolt from a crossbow. The whale flinched and ran. The rope took up. Coil upon coil, it turned out of the boat, feeding through the groove in the gunwale. Suddenly, a tangle stuck in the groove and the rope went taut; the running whale began to tow the boat along. The litter stuffing the hole in the floorboards came bursting out. Ahab bent to free the snagged rope—he did free it, too—but as it began to run out again, a flying coil caught Ahab round the neck and, lifting him bodily, carried him away— no scream, no cry, no word—over the prow and into the wake of the whale. Every metre of hemp rope paid out without Moby Dick slowing his run. The lump of metal which should have pinned the rope's end to the keel was simply wrenched out of the boat: it killed a man in its path.

The surviving few stood watching the last triumphant flourish of Moby Dick as he dived deep. Then they turned to look for the mothership—and there was no ship left to see.

Three masts alone stuck up out of the water, like the three crosses on Golgotha Hill the day Christ was crucified. On the topmast, Queequeg continued to hammer, hammer, hammer home the flag. His arm swung with the rhythm of a clock's ticking. The mast-head and that hammering arm were the last vestige of the *Pequod* to sink out of sight beneath the waves.

As a ship sinks, the suction is so great that she swallows a portion of sea with her, squirming into her grave, then drawing in the sea-soil over her. The vortex created by the sinking *Pequod* drew the last surviving whale-boat under the waves. The group of men standing huddled within it disappeared, like a bunch of flowers thrown into a grave.

The vortex drew me, too. Closer and closer to the churning maelstrom, I slipped over the surface of the sea, like Odysseus sucked towards Charybdis. It seemed I was to spend my eternity among the cabins and companionways of the sunken *Pequod*.

But the whirlpool stopped turning, the water calmed.

With a sudden rush, something white came up beneath me and struck me a shuddering blow as it leapt obliquely out of the water.

No, it was not Moby Dick, nor a tiger shark closing for the kill. It was Queequeg's coffin, sunbleached to white, hammered shut so that air was trapped inside. It bobbed alongside me, a lifebuoy thrown out by the dying ship. I dragged myself across it, drew my hands and feet on to its long lid, and floated away from my shipmates, from my ship, from the longitude and latitude of Ahab's last battle.

For two days the sharks closed their mouths, the sea-hawks turned aside their blood-red beaks. I lived on—I alone—floating on the lid of Queequeg's coffin, as though by some oversight of the gods. I could even hear, as if through the coffin lid, Queequeg's calm, soothing voice: '*Die another day . . . die another day.*' Then a worn sail showed over the rim of the wet world, and a tall hull came tacking to and fro, to and fro in my direction. The ship's yard-arms were crowded with look-outs, like berries on a bare tree, and the flag was American.

It astonished me, those look-outs crowing, fingers pointing excitedly. Was I so loved and missed that this ship had come looking for me, just for me?

But, of course, it was not me they were looking for: I was a bitter disappointment to them, though they took me aboard and treated me with Christian kindness. It was the whaler *Rachel*, you see, still combing the sea for her captain's lost son. Instead of him, they found me. And that is why I am alive today.

Epilogue

I LIVE inland now. There's a whale out there in the sea, as white as a ghost, and I prefer not to think of it. It haunts me on winter nights, when the sky moves like a tumbling grey sea and my bed holds no more comfort than the lid of a coffin. Somewhere out there, in the oceans, lives a great white winter of a whale, and I shiver at the thought of it.

Once I saw a woman standing on the crest of a hill, with a young boy in her arms, looking out to sea. We did not speak. What could I have said to them? Besides, there are many such women, many such seaside hills.

I live inland now; far from ships and friendships; as far from the past as memories allow; far from the sight and sound of the sea and the beasts which rightfully possess it.